# MASTER THE HEBREW ALPHABET

## A Handwriting Practice Workbook

Perfect your calligraphy skills and dominate the Hebraic script

by Lang Workbooks

**Important Legal Information:**

This workbook is a labor of love. Accordingly, if you are a teacher, a student of Hebrew, or homeschooling your children, *I grant you the non-commercial right to photocopy any part of this workbook for your own, or your students, personal use.*

All further rights are reserved © 2019.
ISBN: 9781691222148

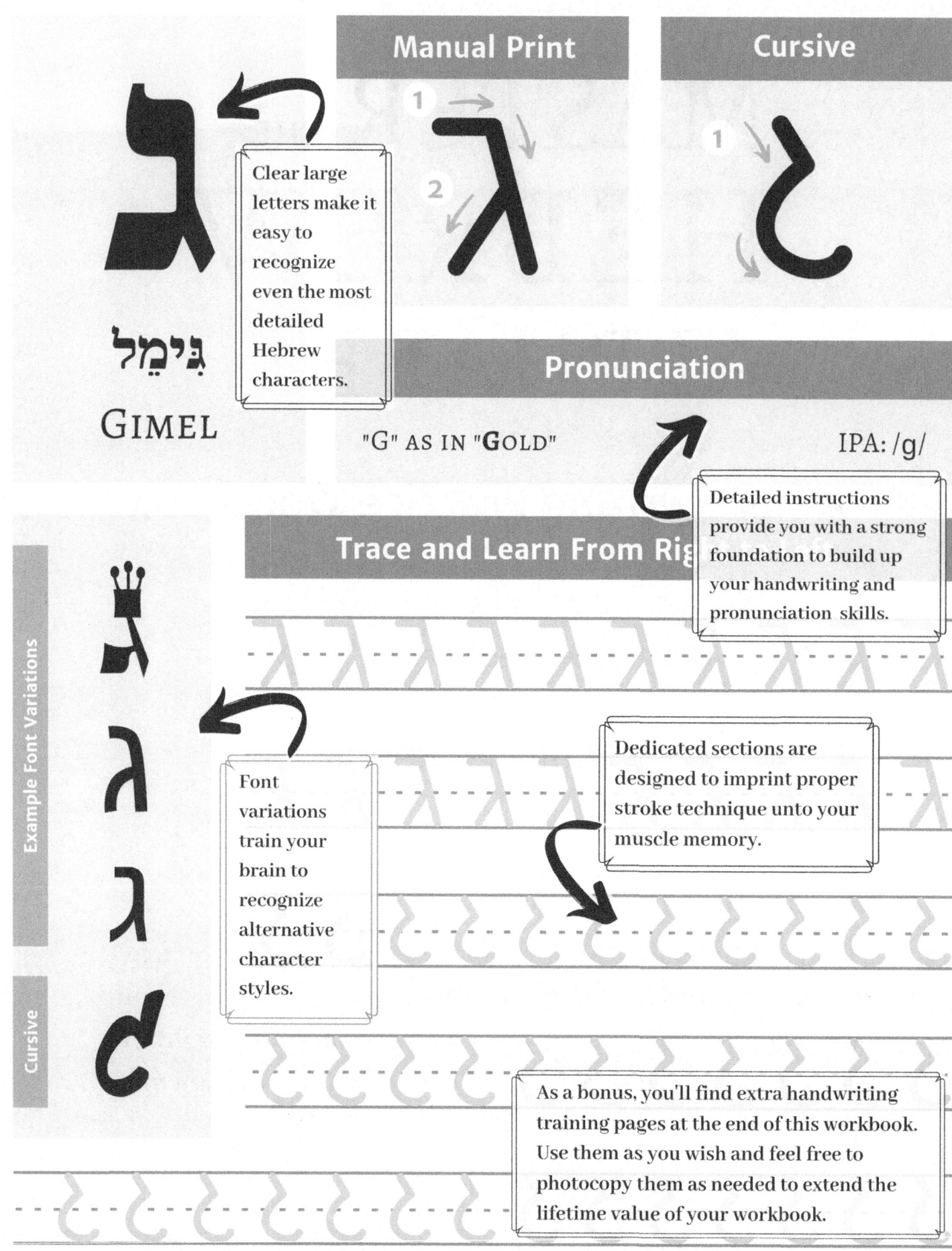

# Workbook Index

| | | | | | |
|---|---|---|---|---|---|
| | INSTRUCTIONS | 2 | מ | MEM | 52 |
| א | ALEPH | 4 | ם | MEM SOFIT | 55 |
| בּ | BET | 7 | נ | NUN | 58 |
| ב | VET | 10 | ן | NUN SOFIT | 61 |
| ג | GIMEL | 13 | ס | SAMEKH | 64 |
| ד | DALET | 16 | ע | 'AYIN | 67 |
| ה | HE | 19 | פּ | PEY | 70 |
| ו | VAV | 22 | פ | FEY | 73 |
| ז | ZAYIN | 25 | ף | PEY SOFIT | 76 |
| ח | HET | 28 | צ | TSADE | 79 |
| ט | TET | 31 | ץ | TSADE SOFIT | 82 |
| י | YOD | 34 | ק | QOF | 85 |
| כּ | KAF | 37 | ר | RESH | 88 |
| כ | KHAF | 40 | שׁ | SHIN | 91 |
| ך | KAF SOFIT | 43 | שׂ | SIN | 94 |
| ך | KHAF SOFIT | 46 | תּ | TAV (DAGESH) | 97 |
| ל | LAMED | 49 | ת | TAV | 100 |

VOWLES PRACTICE WITH REFERENCE CHART        103 - 111

BONUS TRAINING PAGES        112 - 120

א

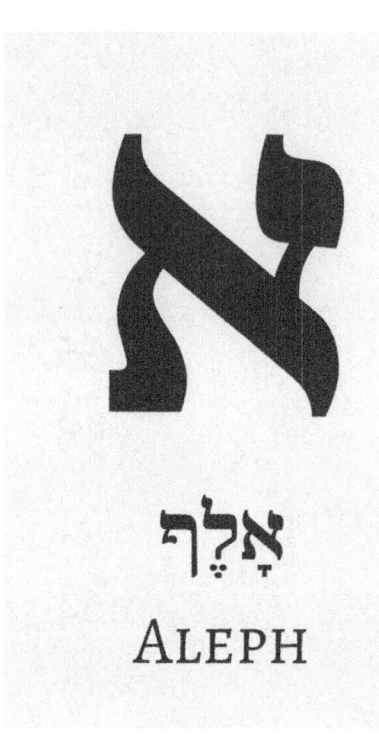

אָלֶף

ALEPH

## Manual Print

## Cursive

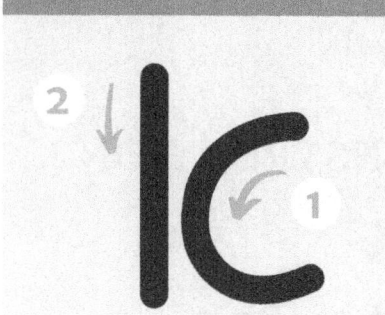

## Pronunciation

ALEPH IS A SILENT LETTER

IPA: /ʔ/

Example Font Variations

א

א

א

Cursive

## Trace and Learn From Right to Left

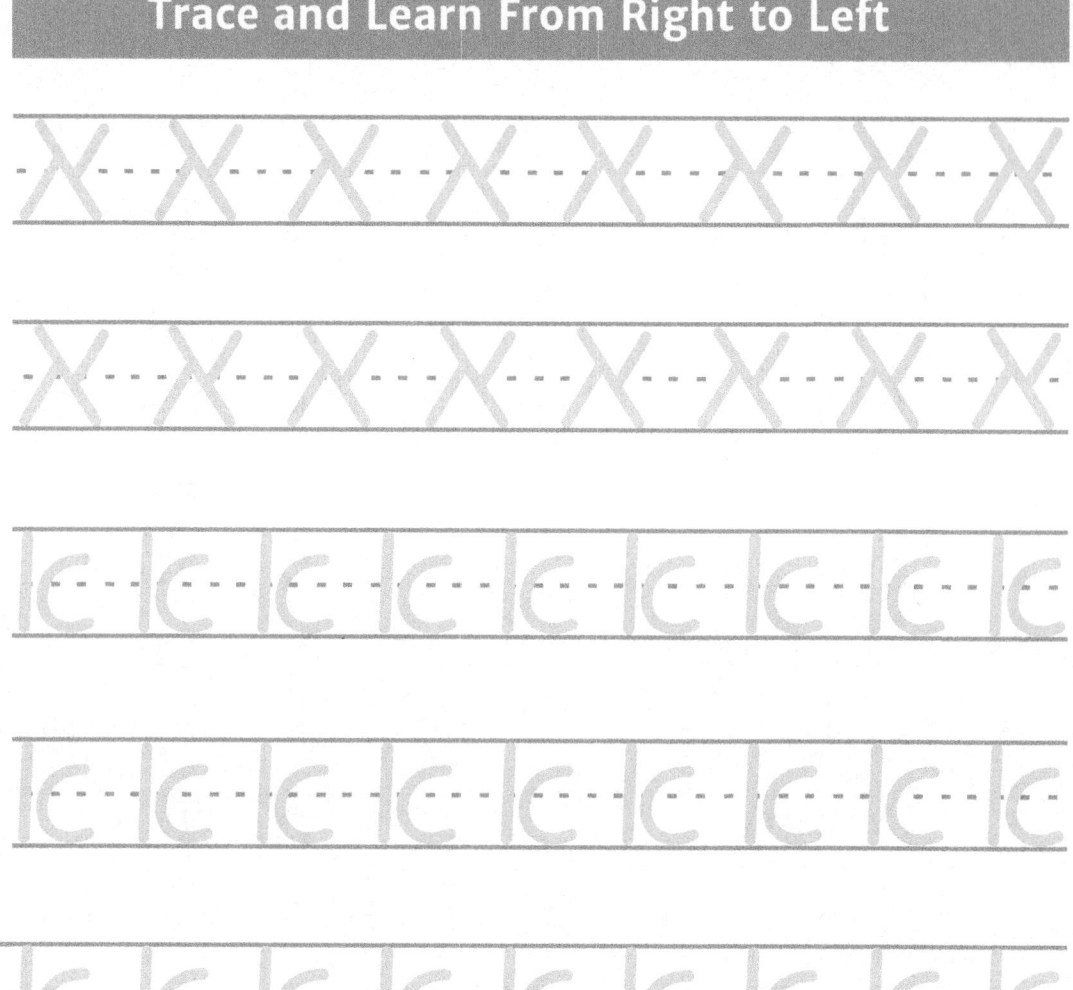

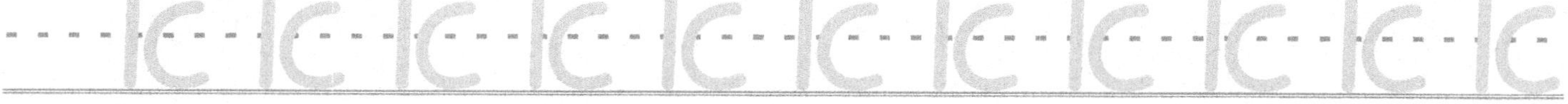

k k k k k k k k k k

## Manual Print

## Cursive

בֵּית

BET

## Pronunciation

"B" AS IN "**B**ILL"  IPA: /b/

## Trace and Learn From Right to Left

**Example Font Variations**

**Cursive**

7

ב ב ב ב ב ב ב ב ב ב ב ב

בֵּית
Vet

## Manual Print
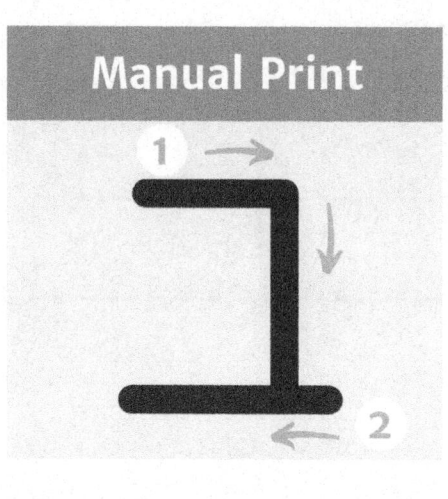

## Cursive

## Pronunciation

"V" as in "Violin"   IPA: /v/

## Trace and Learn From Right to Left

ح ح ح ح ح ح ح ح ح ح ح ح

דָּלֶת

DALET

## Manual Print

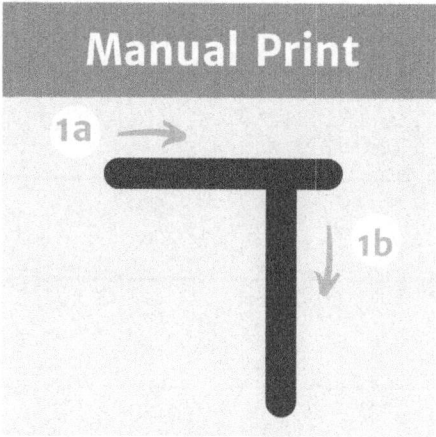

## Cursive

## Pronunciation

"D" AS IN "DICE"　　　　　　　　　　IPA: /d/

## Trace and Learn From Right to Left

Example Font Variations

Cursive

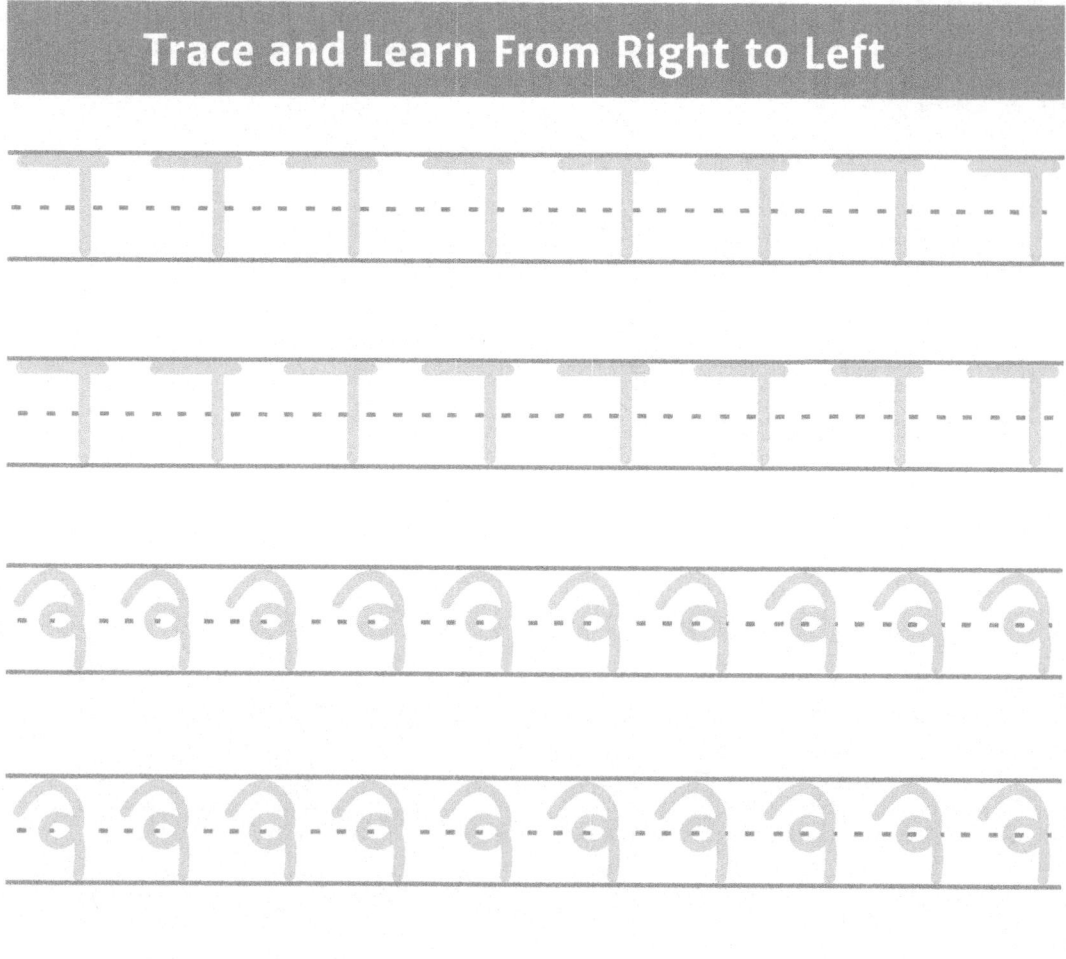

16

## Manual Print

1a, 1b, 2

## Cursive

1, 2

הֵא

He

## Pronunciation

"H" AS IN "**H**ELP"  IPA: /h/

**Example Font Variations**

**Cursive**

## Trace and Learn From Right to Left

וָו

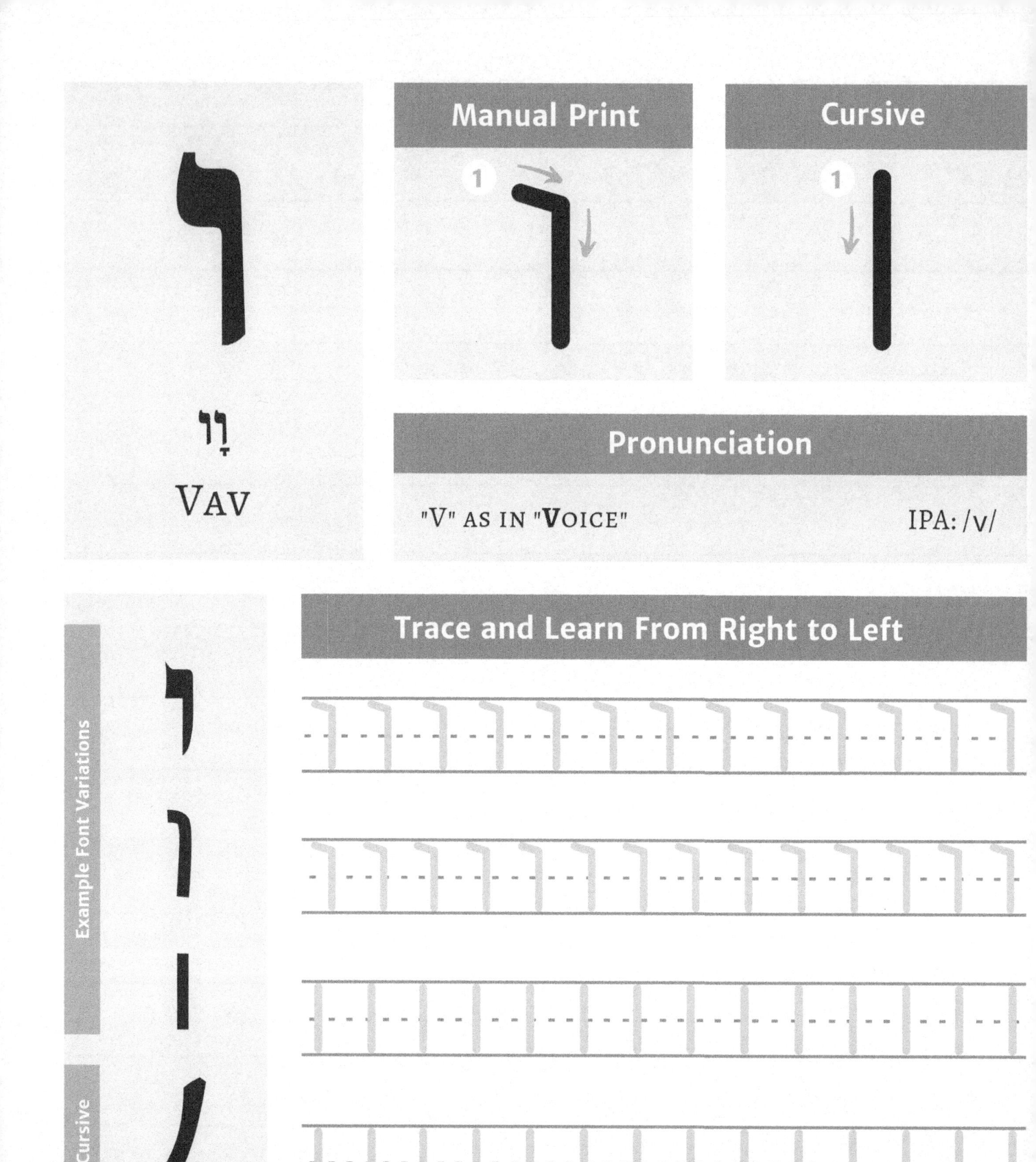

**VAV**

## Manual Print

## Cursive

## Pronunciation

"V" AS IN "**V**OICE"  IPA: /v/

**Example Font Variations**

**Cursive**

## Trace and Learn From Right to Left

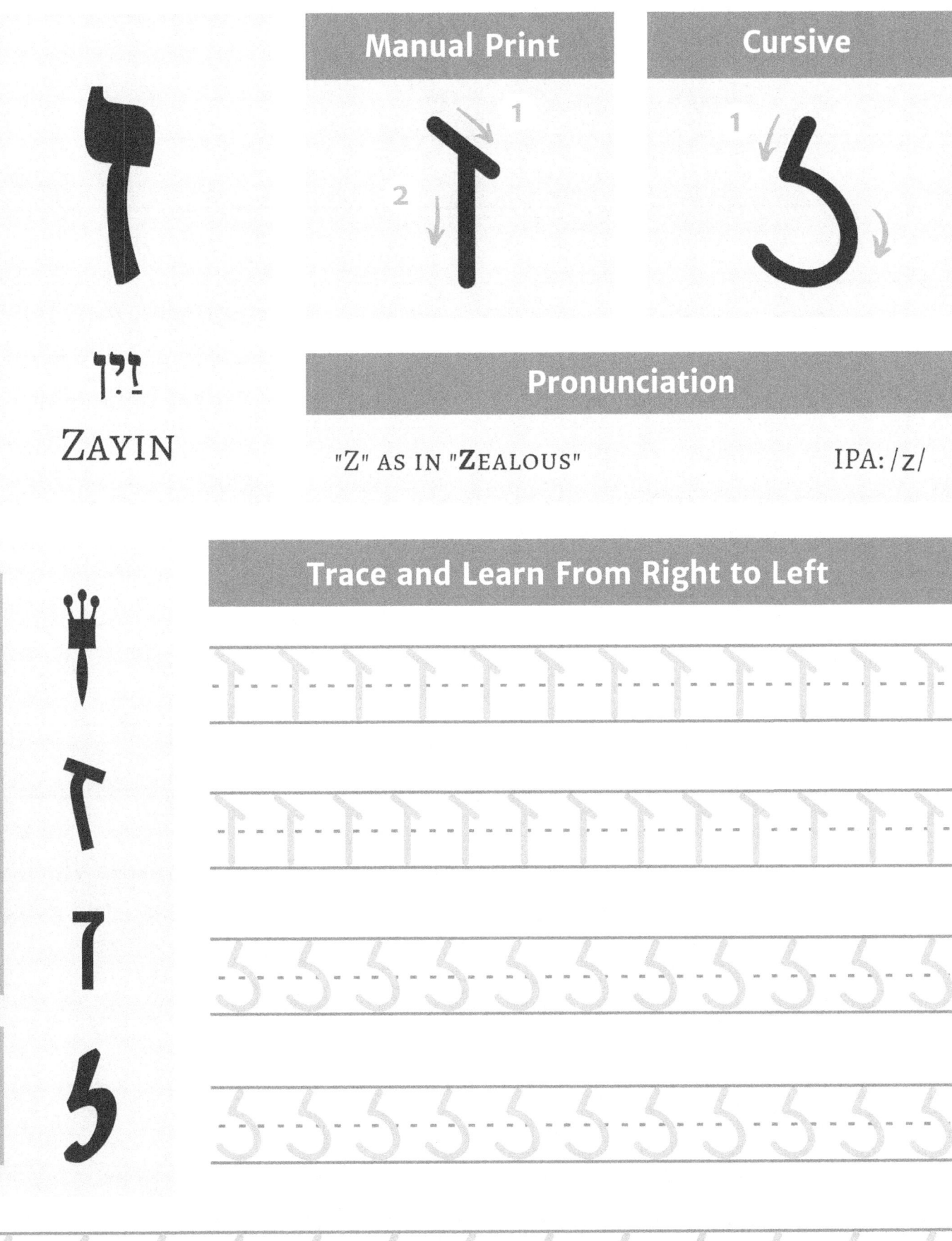

5 5 5 5 5 5 5 5 5 5 5 5 5 5 5

ח

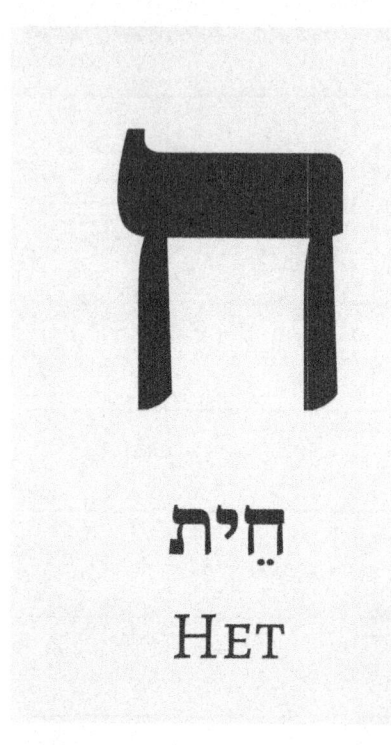

חֵית

HET

## Manual Print

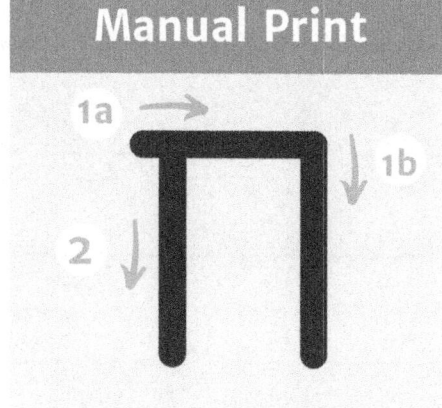

## Cursive

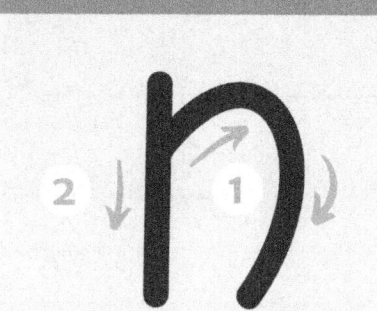

## Pronunciation

"CH" AS IN THE GERMAN NAME "BA**CH**" IPA: /x/

Example Font Variations

ח

ח

ח

Cursive

ח

## Trace and Learn From Right to Left

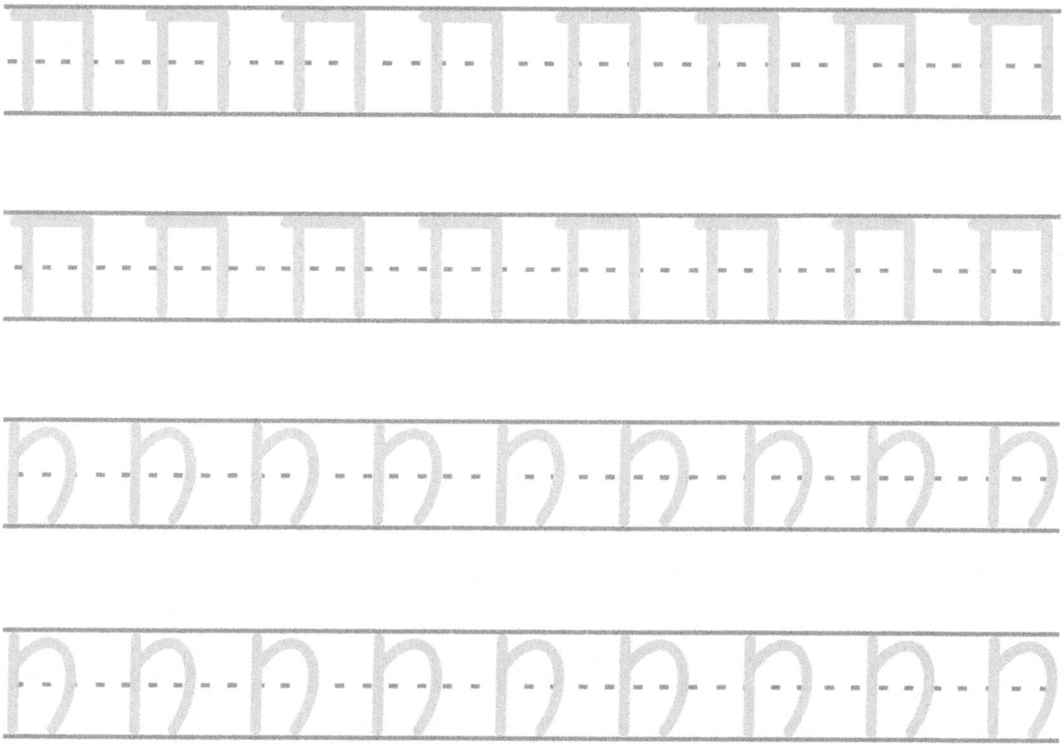

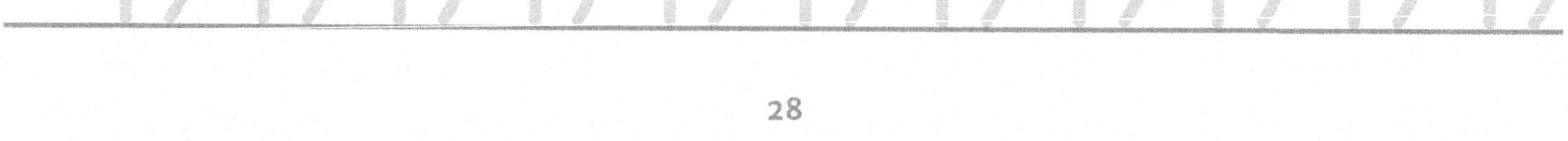

ክ ክ ክ ክ ክ ክ ክ ክ ክ ክ ክ ክ

## Manual Print

## Cursive

כּ
KAF

## Pronunciation

"K" AS IN "KILOMETER"　　　　IPA: /k/

## Trace and Learn From Right to Left

Example Font Variations

Cursive

37

בּ בּ בּ בּ בּ בּ בּ בּ בּ בּ בּ בּ

בּ

בּ

בּ

בּ

בּ

בּ

בּ

בּ

## כ
### כָף
### KHAF

**Manual Print**

**Cursive**

**Pronunciation**

"CH" AS IN THE GERMAN NAME "BACH"   IPA: /x/

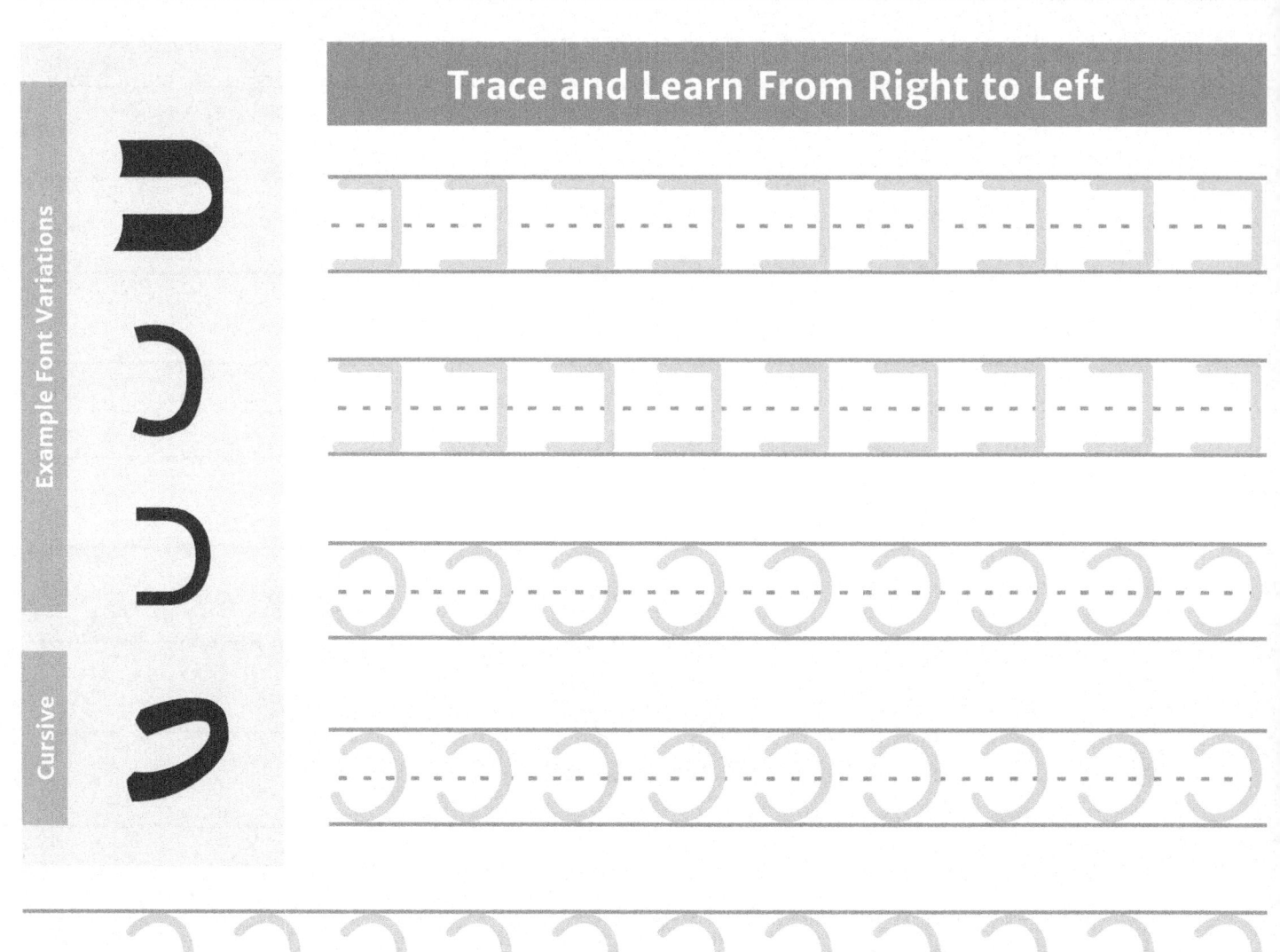

**Trace and Learn From Right to Left**

*Example Font Variations*

*Cursive*

## כַּף סוֹפִית
### Kaf Sofit

**Manual Print** | **Cursive**

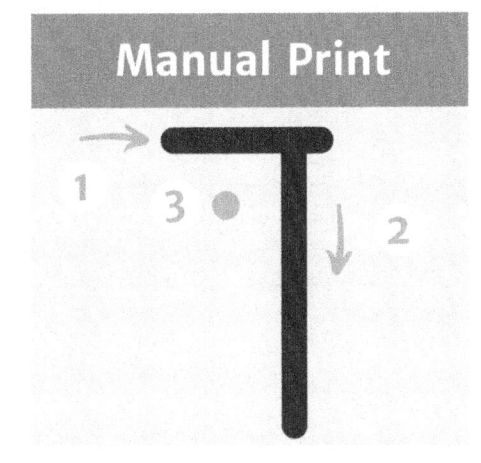

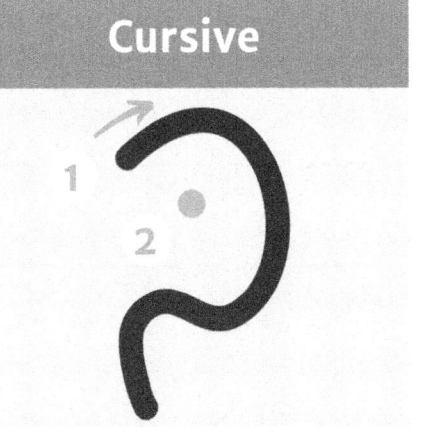

**Pronunciation**

"K" AS IN "**K**ILOMETER"  IPA: /k/

**Trace and Learn From Right to Left**

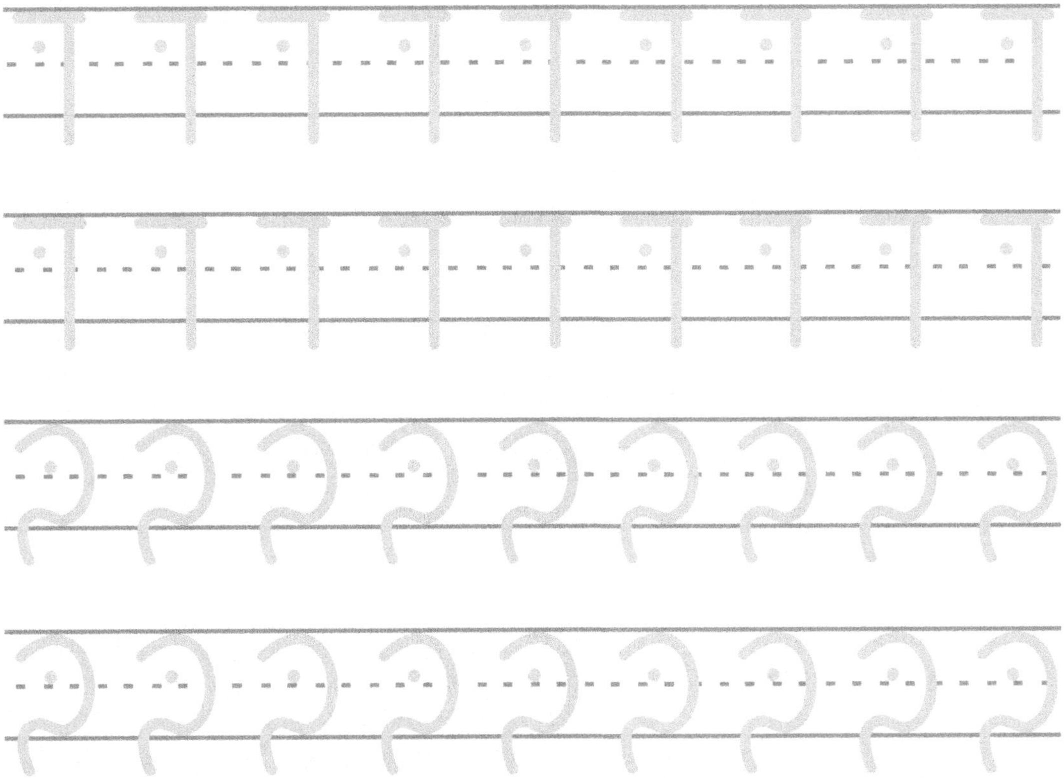

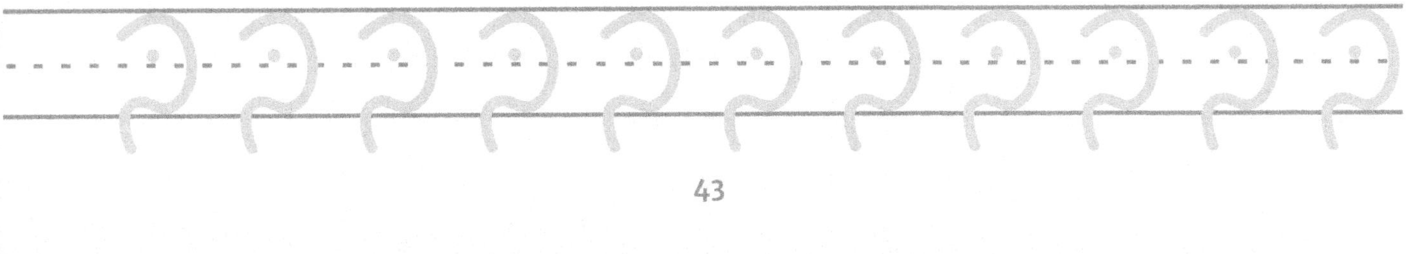

TTTTTTTTTTTT

## כַּף סוֹפִית
## Khaf Sofit

### Manual Print
### Cursive

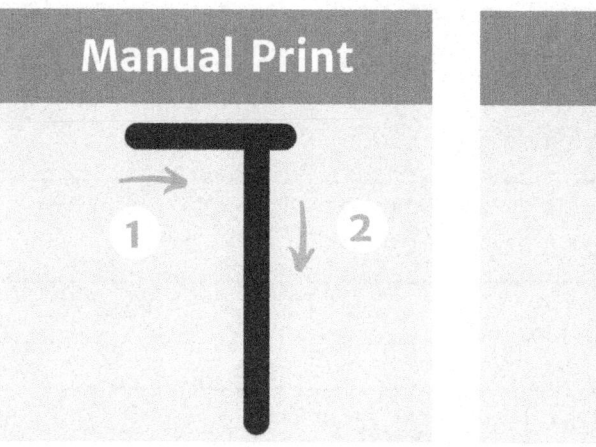

### Pronunciation
"CH" as in the German name "Ba**ch**"   IPA: /x/

### Trace and Learn From Right to Left

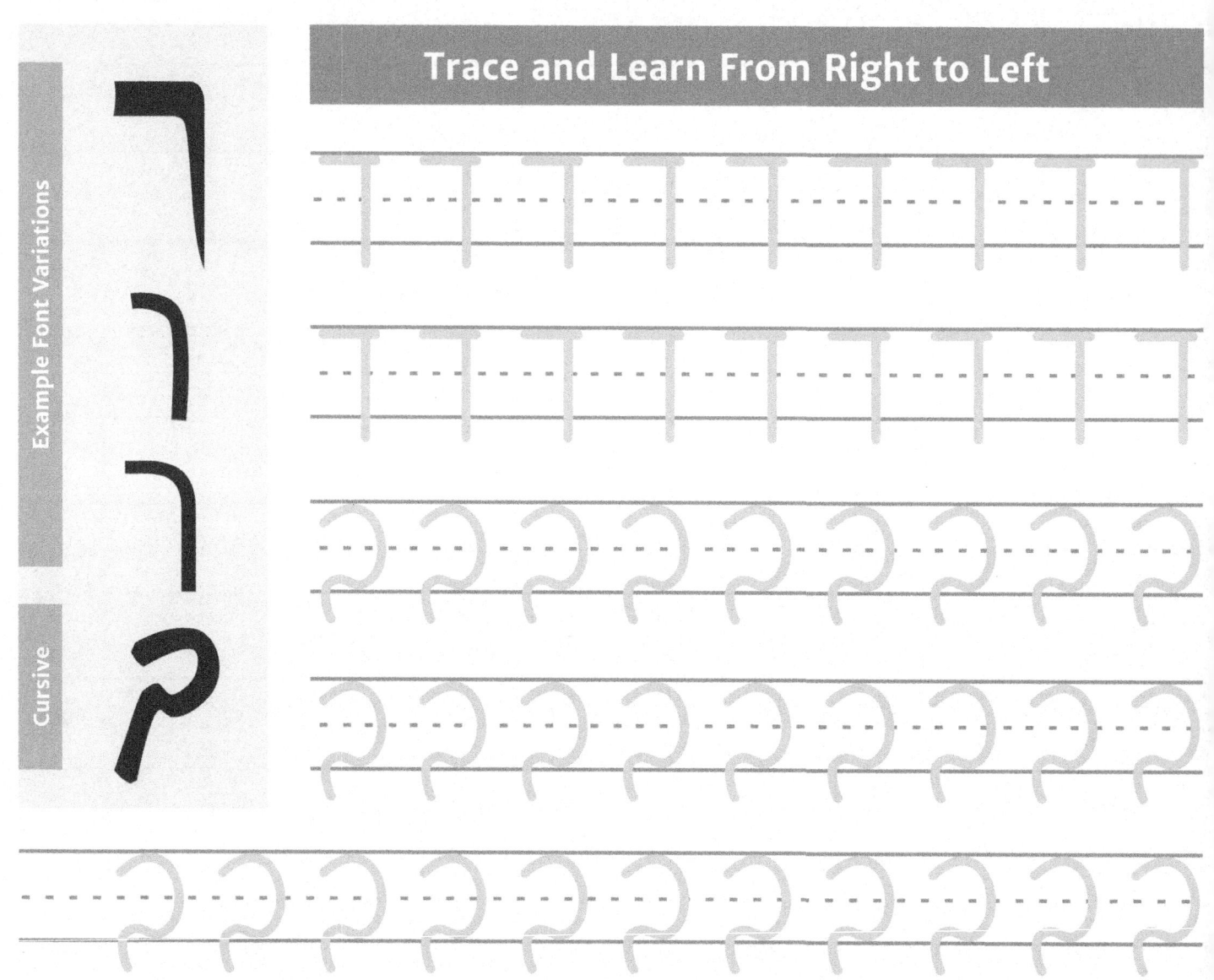

TTTTTTTTTTTTTT

## LAMED

לָמֶד

**Manual Print**

**Cursive**

**Pronunciation**

"L" AS IN "LIFE"

IPA: /l/

**Trace and Learn From Right to Left**

49

ל ל ל ל ל ל ל ל ל ל ל ל

ל

ל

ל

ל

ל

ל

ל

ל

51

מֵם
MEM

## Manual Print
## Cursive

## Pronunciation

"M" AS IN "MILK"  IPA: /m/

**Example Font Variations**

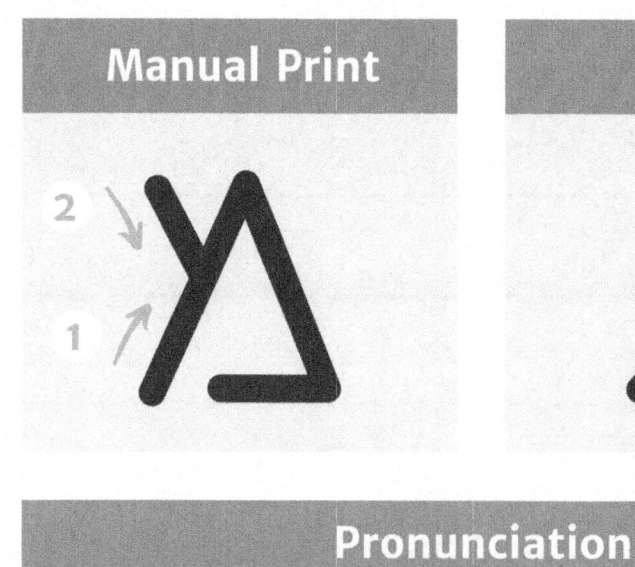

**Cursive**

## Trace and Learn From Right to Left

52

NNNNNNNNNN

## מֵם סוֹפִית
## Mem Sofit

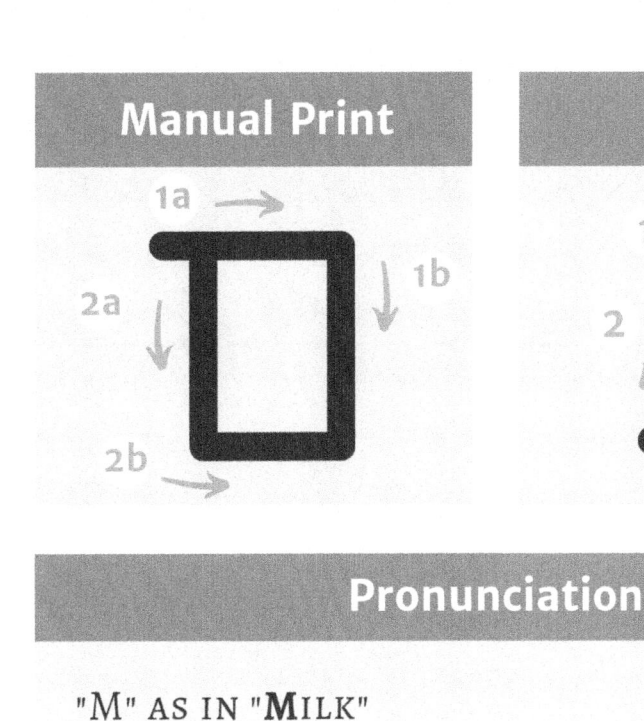

### Manual Print
1a →
1b ↓
2a ↓
2b →

### Cursive
1
2

### Pronunciation
"M" AS IN "MILK"     IPA: /m/

**Example Font Variations**

**Cursive**

### Trace and Learn From Right to Left

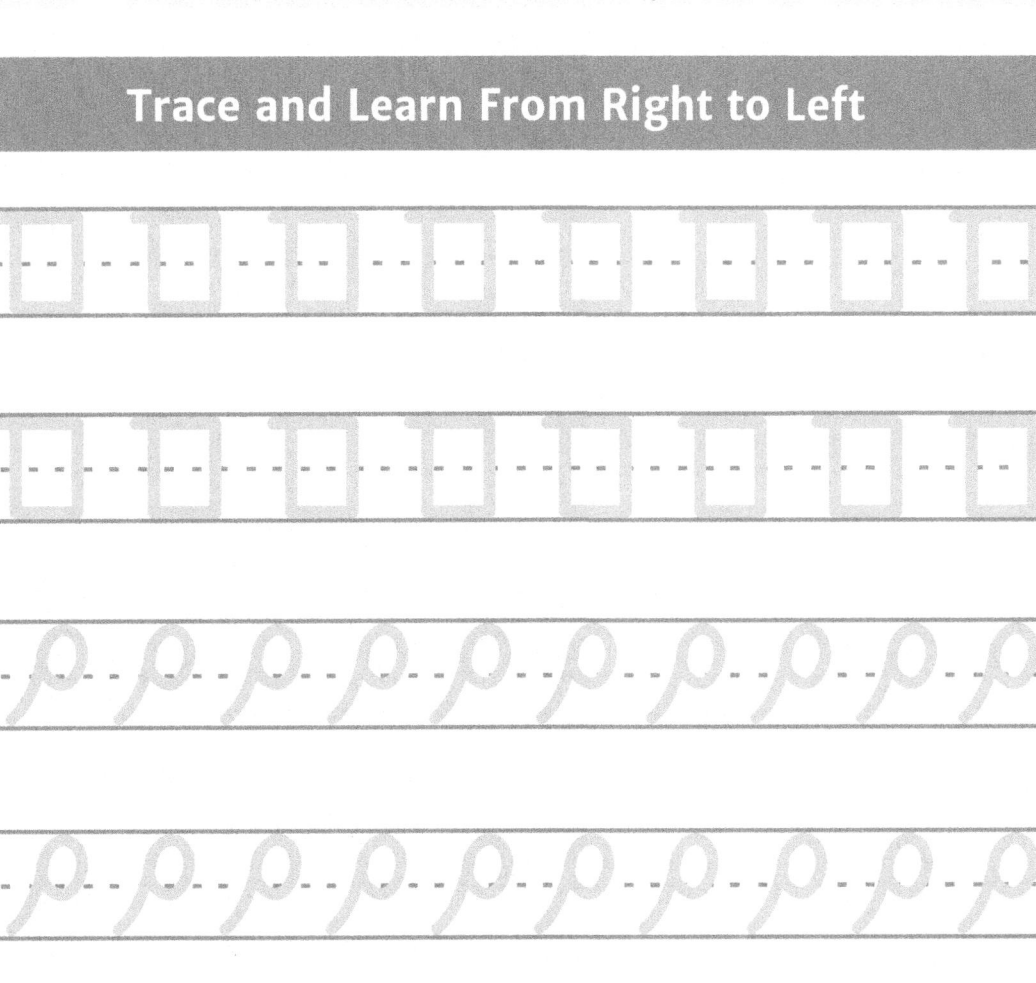

## Manual Print
## Cursive

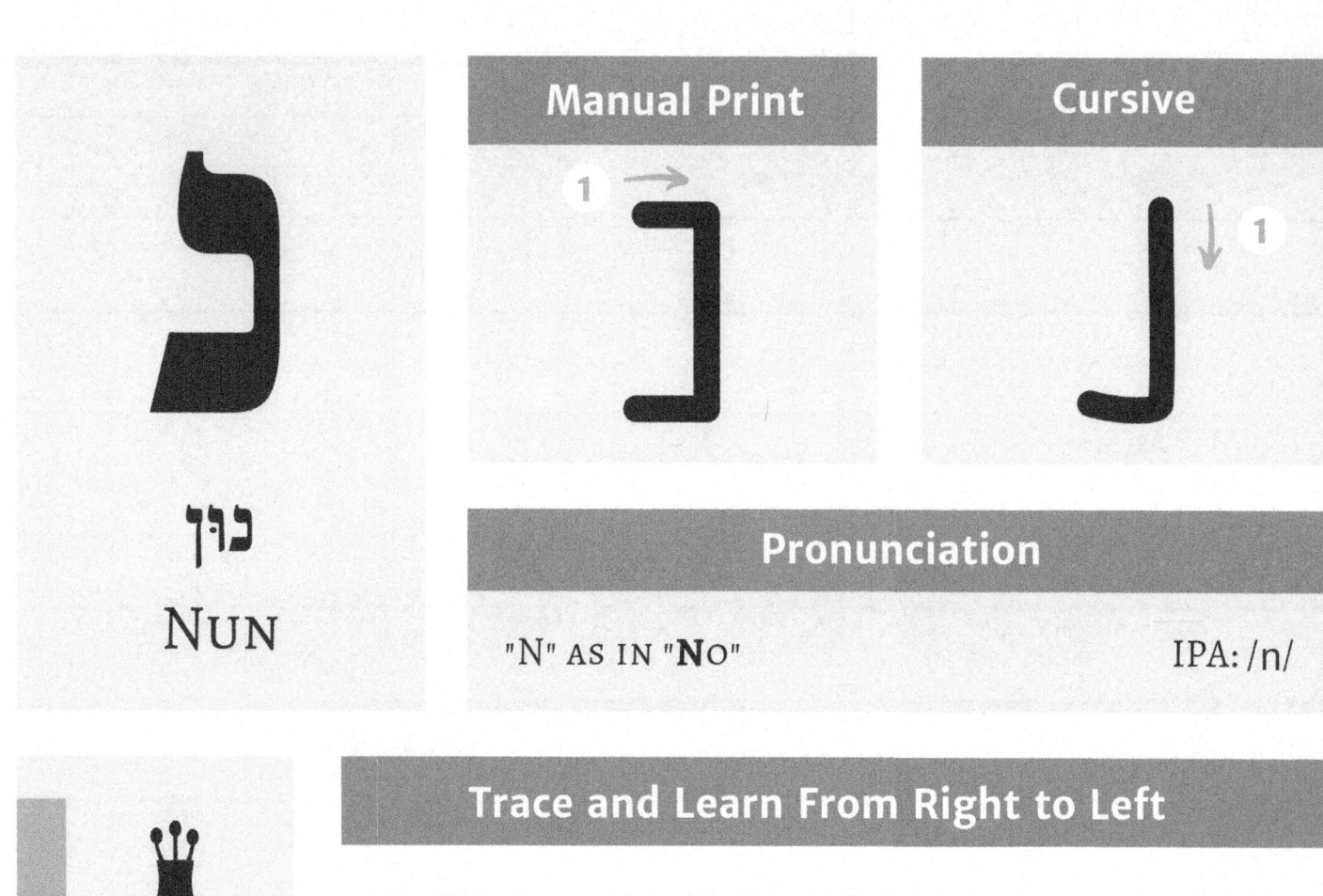

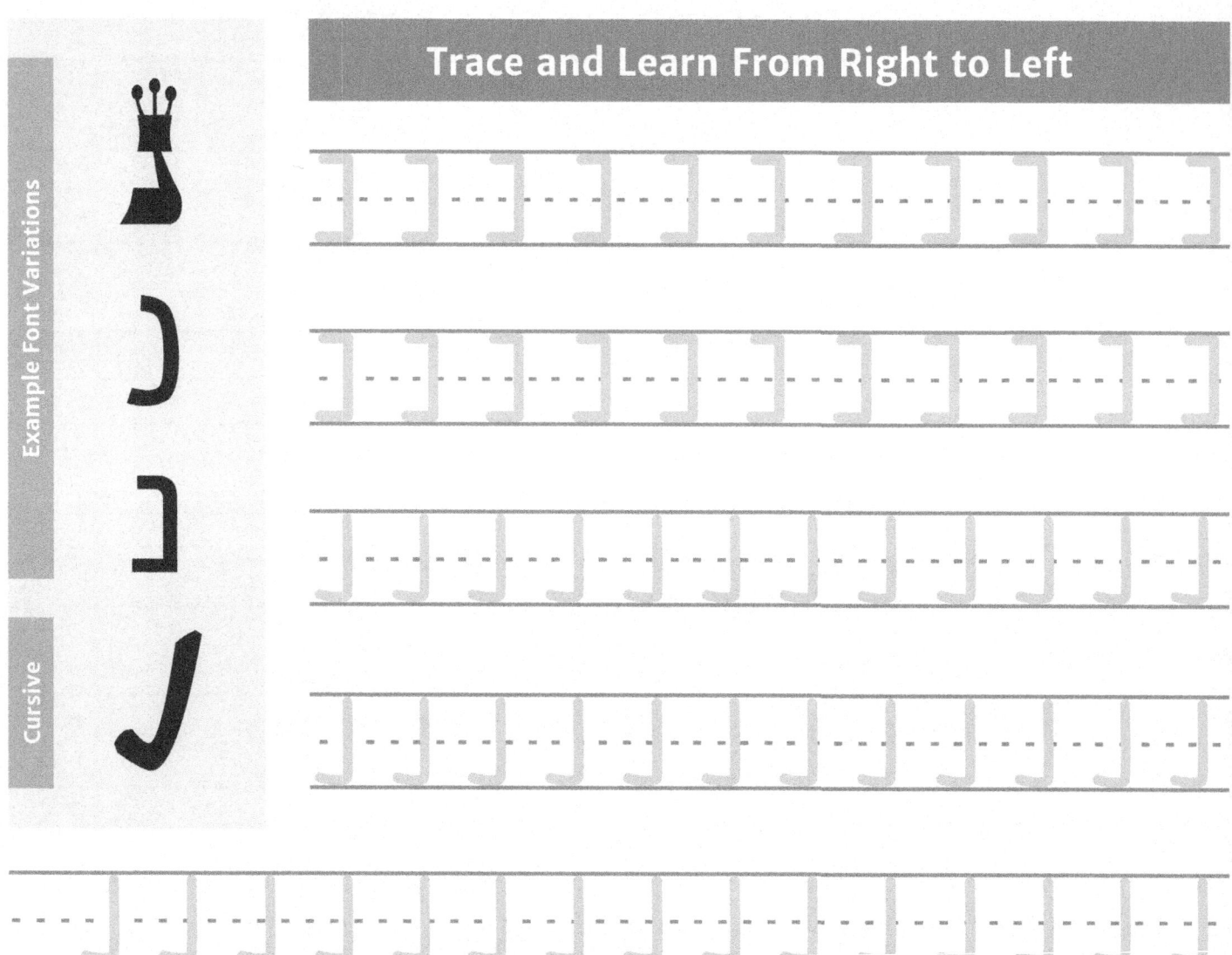

נוּן
NUN

## Pronunciation

"N" AS IN "**N**O"　　　　　IPA: /n/

**Example Font Variations**

**Cursive**

## Trace and Learn From Right to Left

## נון סופית
## Nun Sofit

### Manual Print
### Cursive

### Pronunciation
"N" AS IN "No"  IPA: /n/

### Trace and Learn From Right to Left

ך ך ך ך ך ך ך ך ך ך ך ך ך

ך

ך

ך

ך

ך

ך

ך

ך

ס
סָמֶךְ
SAMEKH

## Manual Print

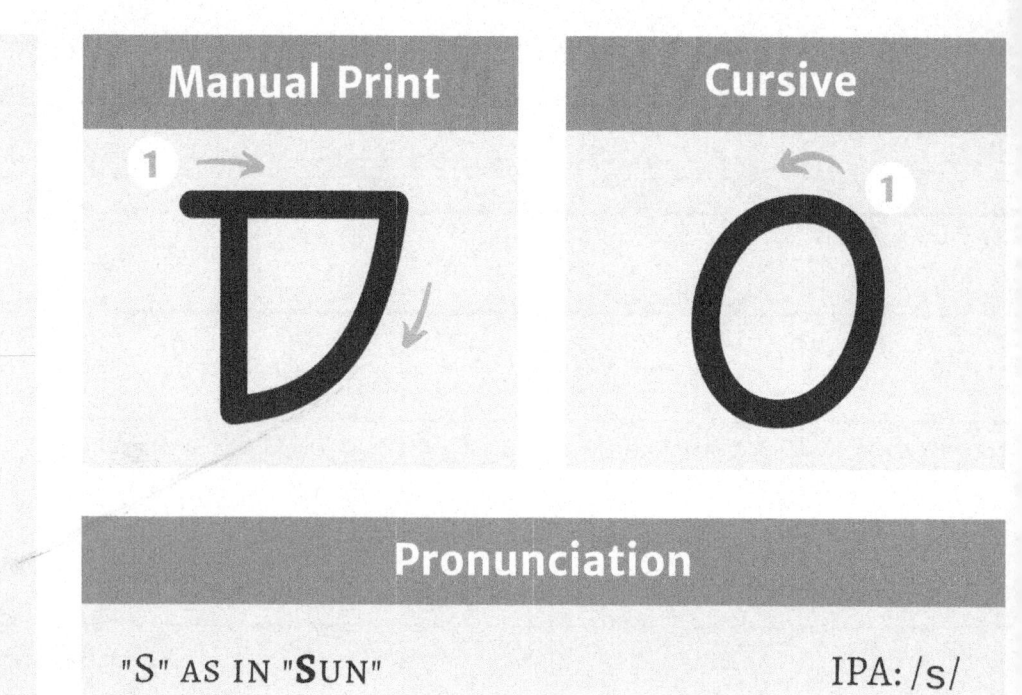

## Cursive

## Pronunciation

"S" AS IN "SUN"  IPA: /s/

**Example Font Variations**

**Cursive**

## Trace and Learn From Right to Left

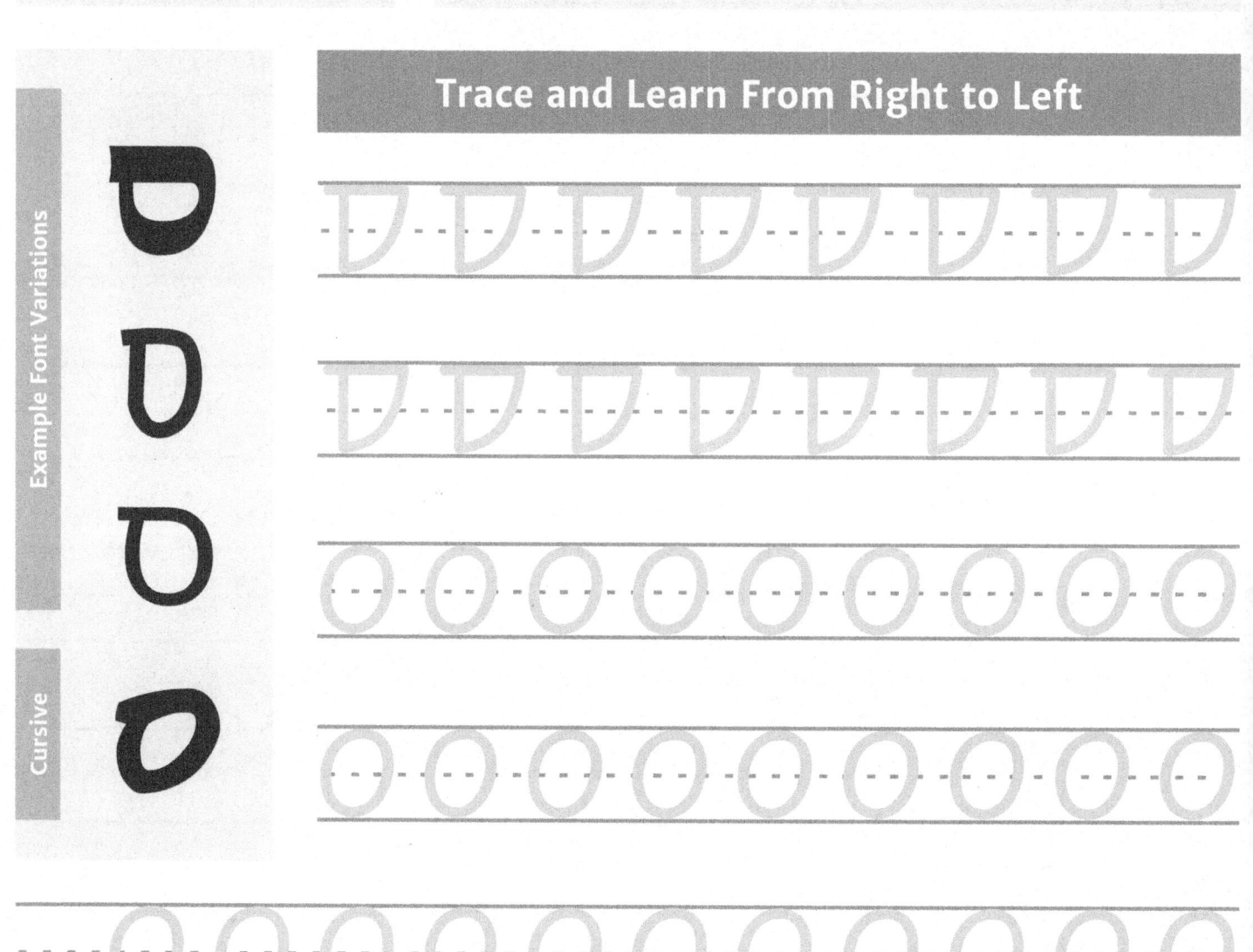

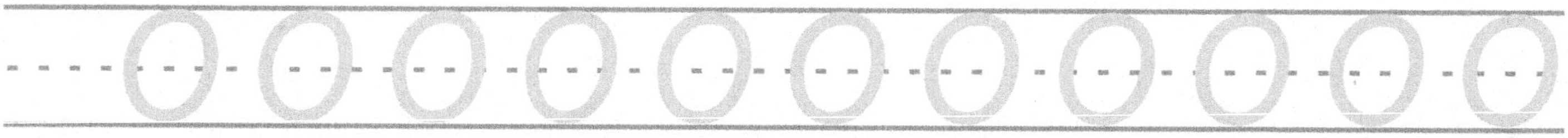

64

סָמֶךְ

'AYIN

## Manual Print

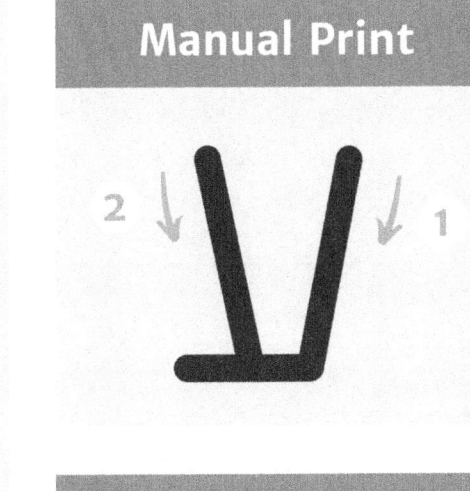

## Cursive

## Pronunciation

'AYIN IS A SILENT LETTER  IPA: /∅/

## Trace and Learn From Right to Left

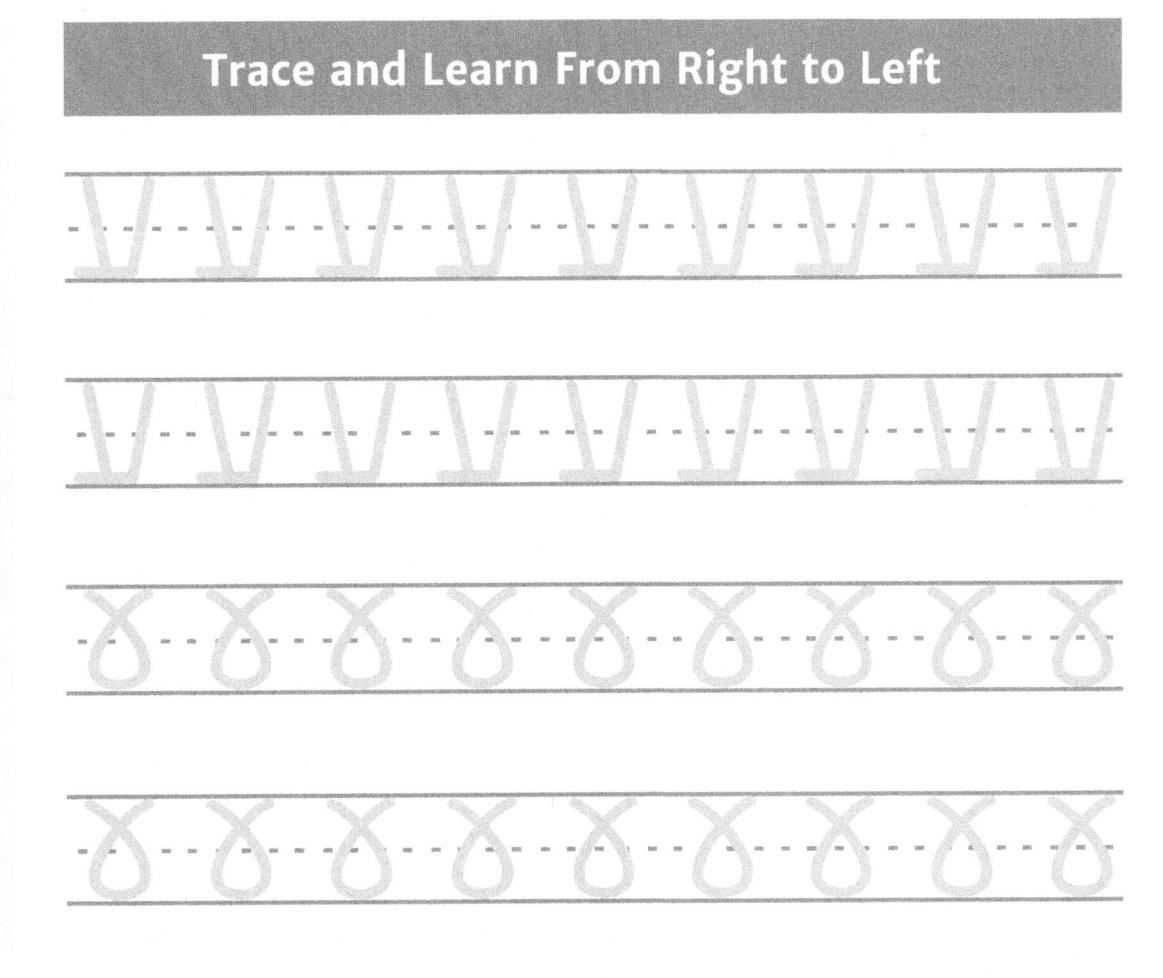

**Example Font Variations**

**Cursive**

67

V V V V V V V V V V V

ɣ ɣ ɣ ɣ ɣ ɣ ɣ ɣ ɣ ɣ ɣ ɣ

ɣ

ɣ

ɣ

ɣ

ɣ

ɣ

ɣ

ɣ

## Manual Print

## Cursive

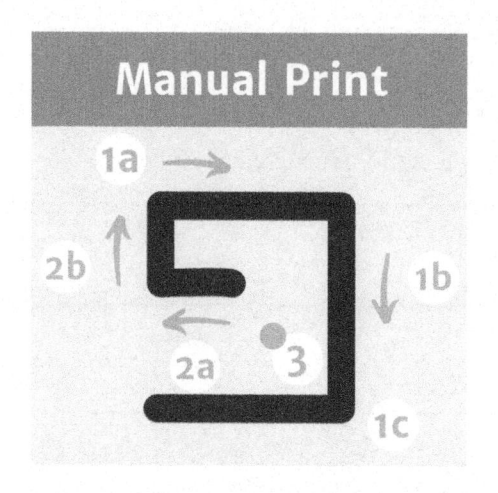

פּ

PEY

## Pronunciation

"P" AS IN "POOL"

IPA: /p/

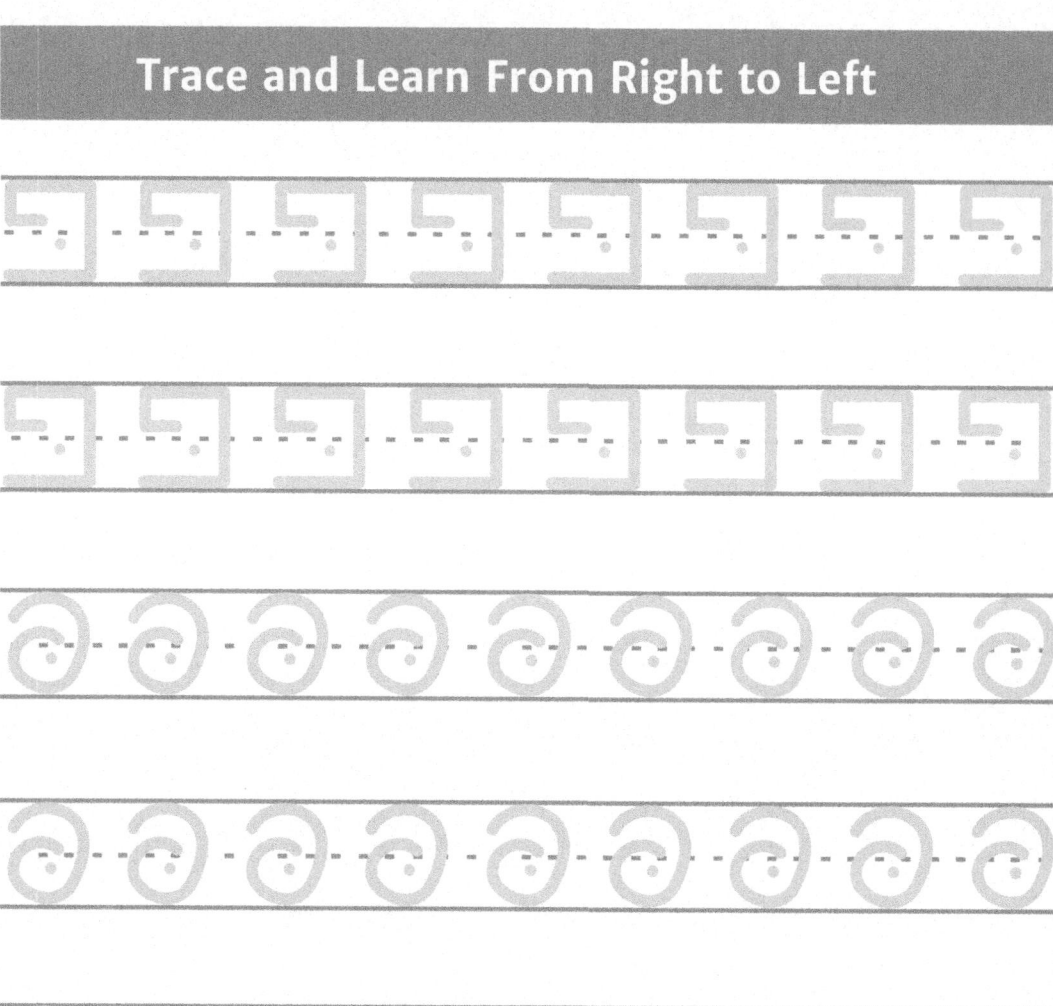

**Example Font Variations**

**Cursive**

## Trace and Learn From Right to Left

70

71

## Manual Print

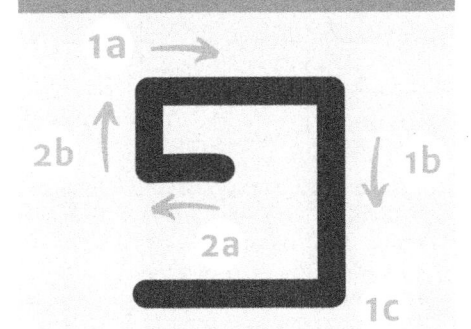

## Cursive

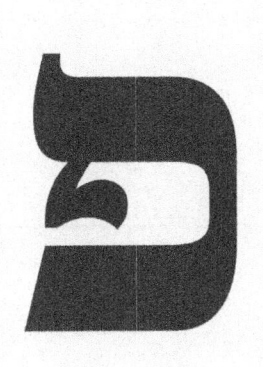

פ

FEY

## Pronunciation

"PH" AS IN "PHONE"  IPA: /f/

## Trace and Learn From Right to Left

**Example Font Variations**

**Cursive**

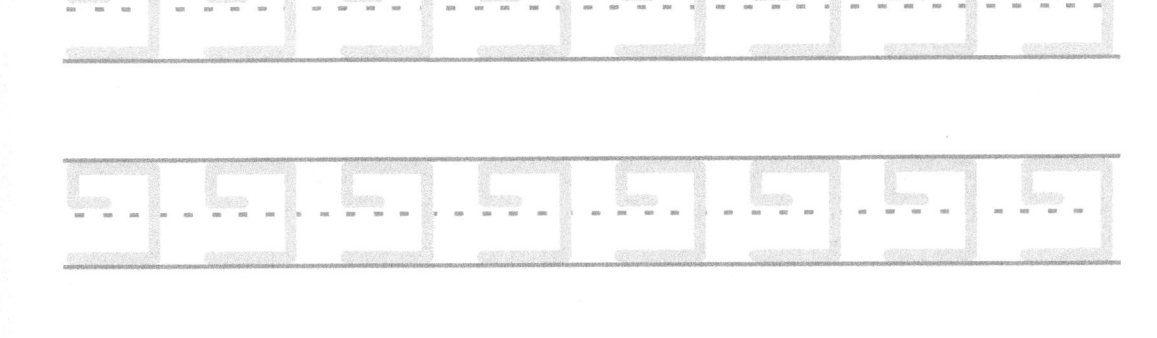

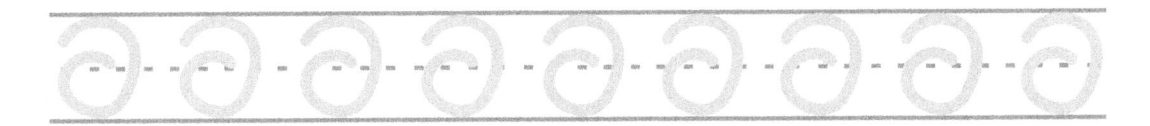

73

ଅ ଅ ଅ ଅ ଅ ଅ ଅ ଅ ଅ ଅ ଅ ଅ

## Pey Sofit

פֵּא סוֹפִית

### Manual Print

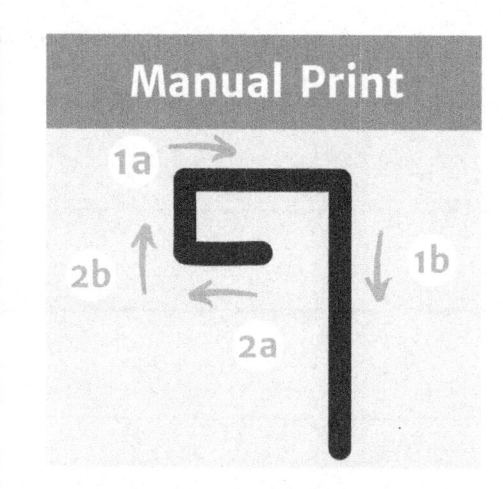

1a, 1b, 2a, 2b

### Cursive

1

### Pronunciation

"PH" AS IN "PHONE"  IPA: /f/

**Example Font Variations**

**Cursive**

### Trace and Learn From Right to Left

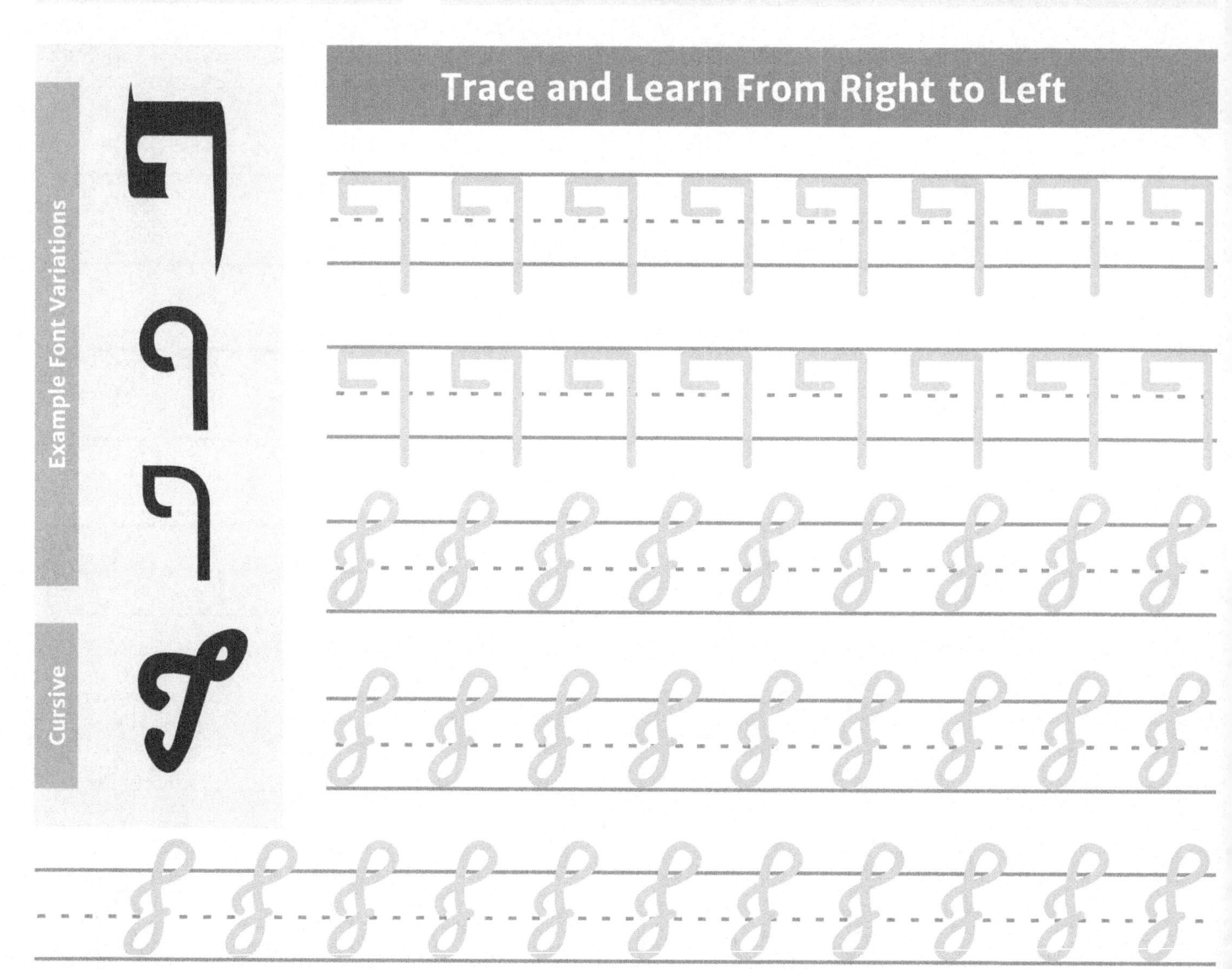

ㄱ ㄱ ㄱ ㄱ ㄱ ㄱ ㄱ ㄱ ㄱ ㄱ ㄱ ㄱ

## Manual Print

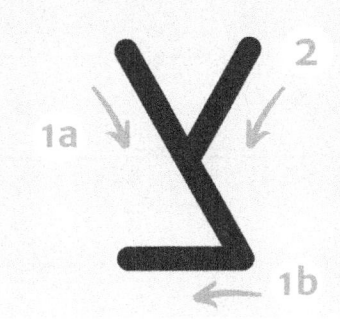

## Cursive

צַדִי

TSADE

## Pronunciation

"Ts" AS IN "NuTS"

IPA: /t͡s/

## Trace and Learn From Right to Left

*Example Font Variations*

*Cursive*

YYYYYYYYYYYYY

3 3 3 3 3 3 3 3 3 3 3 3

## Manual Print

## Cursive

צָדִי סוֹפִית

TSADE SOFIT

## Pronunciation

"TS" AS IN "NUTS"

IPA: /t͡s/

**Example Font Variations**

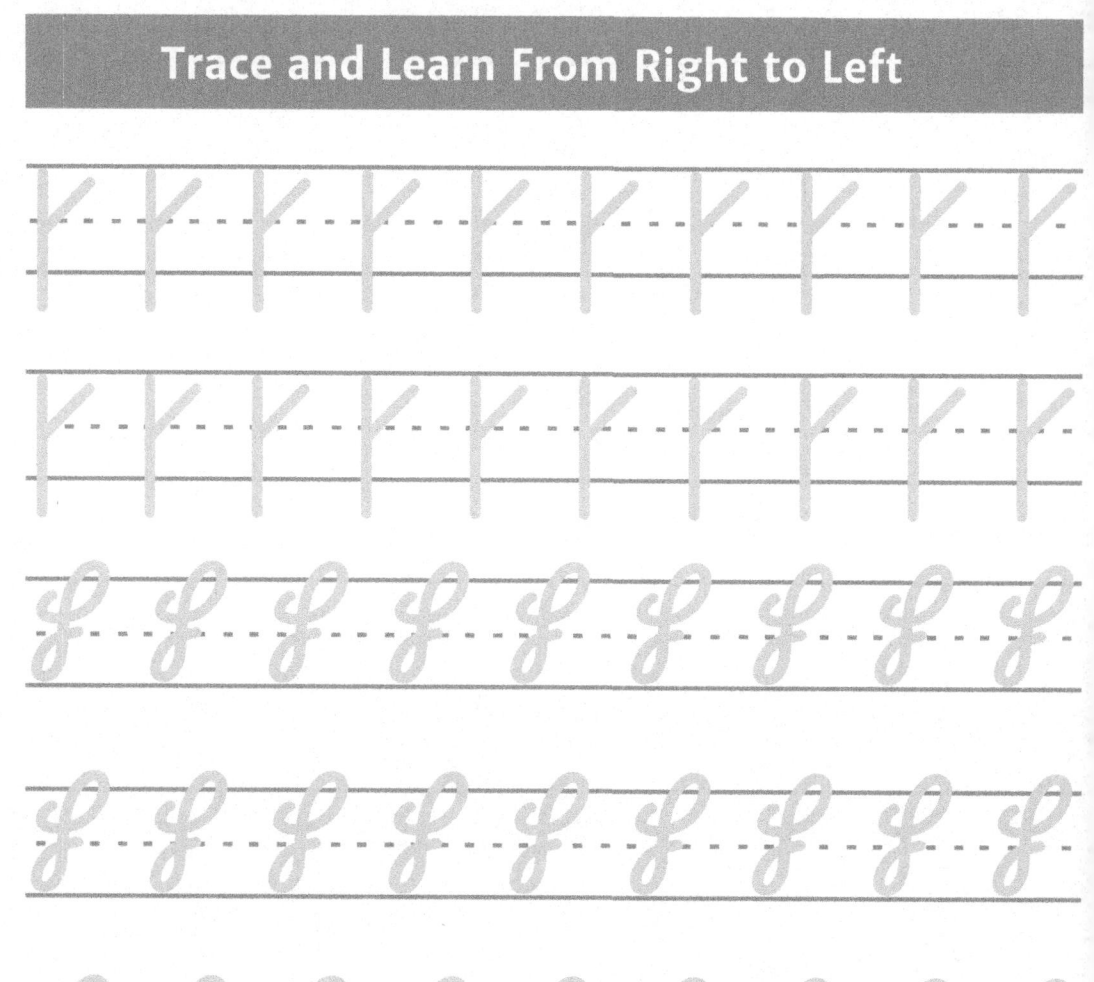

**Cursive**

## Trace and Learn From Right to Left

83

קוֹף
QOF

## Manual Print

## Cursive

## Pronunciation

"C" AS IN "CAR"  IPA: /k/

## Trace and Learn From Right to Left

**Example Font Variations**

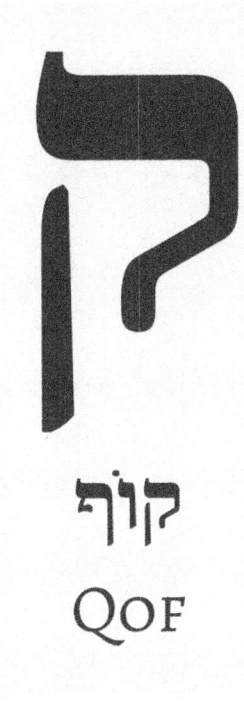

**Cursive**

p p p p p p p p p p p p

## Manual Print

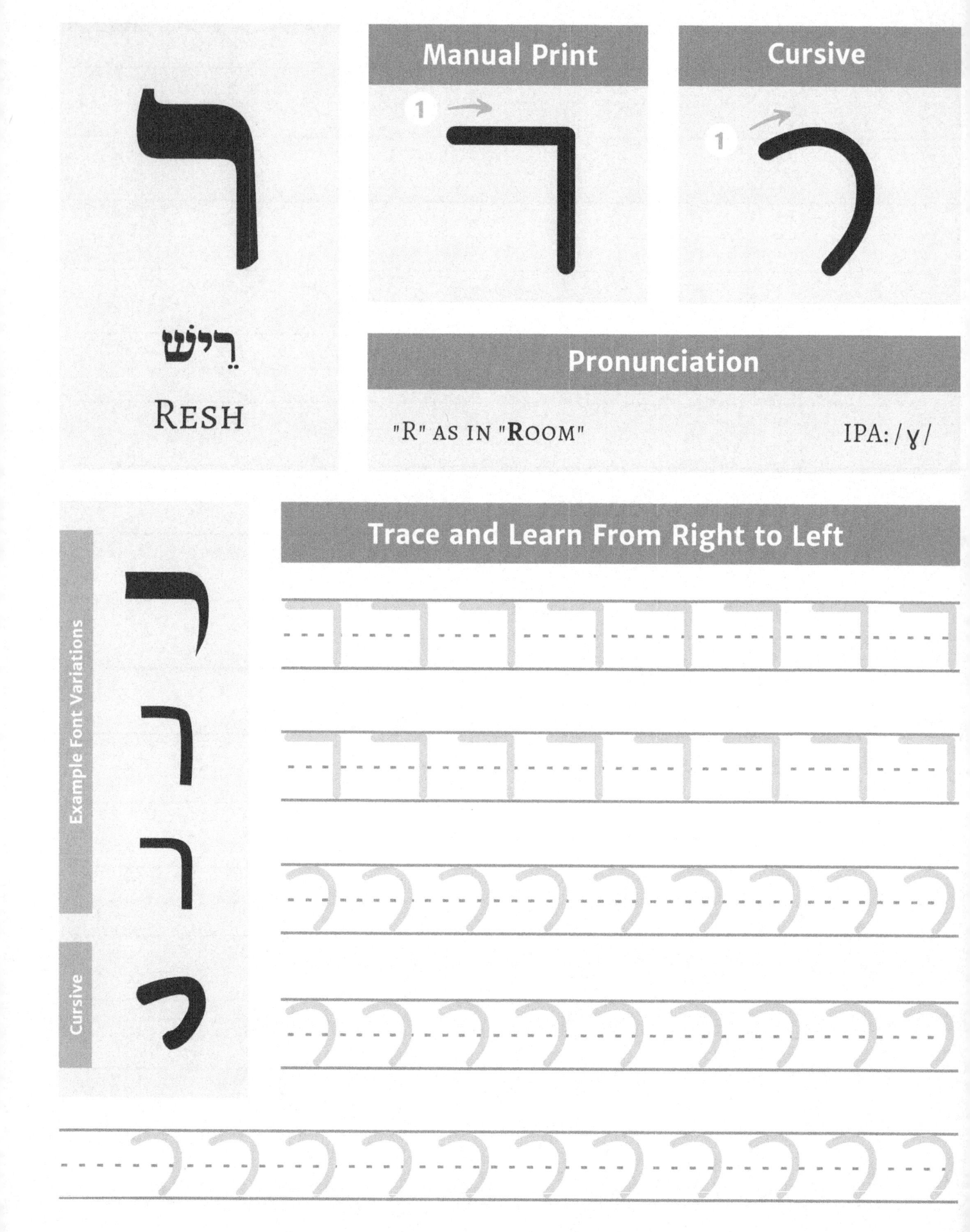

## Cursive

רֵישׁ

RESH

## Pronunciation

"R" AS IN "ROOM"

IPA: /ɣ/

## Trace and Learn From Right to Left

Example Font Variations

Cursive

## Manual Print

## Cursive

שׁין

SHIN

## Pronunciation

"SH" AS IN "SHOULD"  IPA: /ʃ/

## Trace and Learn From Right to Left

Example Font Variations

Cursive

e e e e e e e e e e e e

e

e

e

e

e

e

e

e

## Manual Print

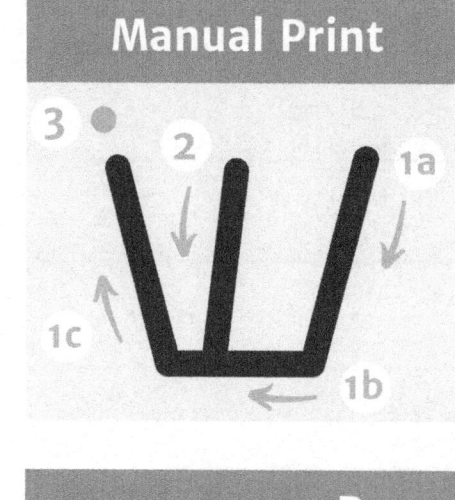

## Cursive

שִׁין

SIN

## Pronunciation

"S" AS IN "SUN"    IPA: /s/

**Example Font Variations**

**Cursive**

## Trace and Learn From Right to Left

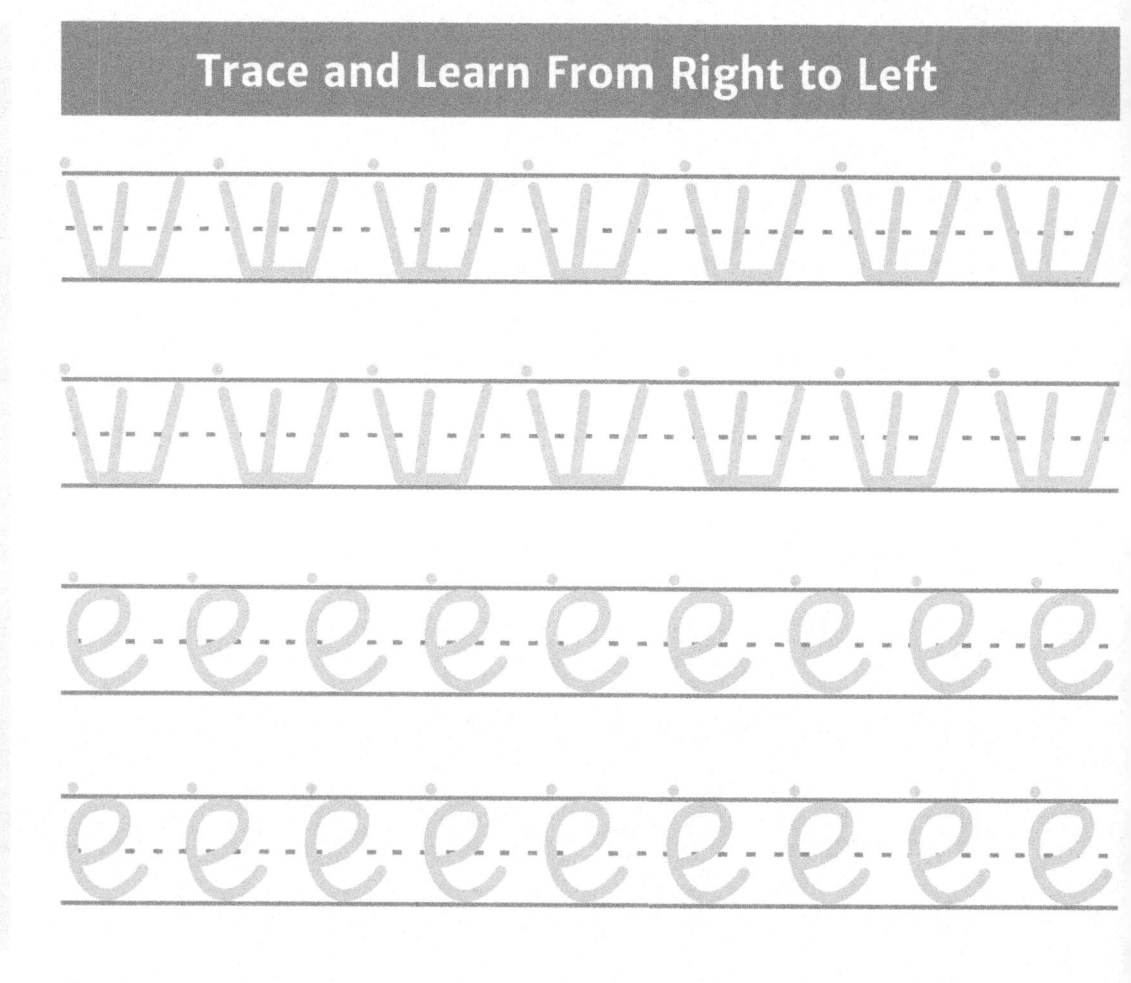

eeeeeeeeeeeeee

## Manual Print

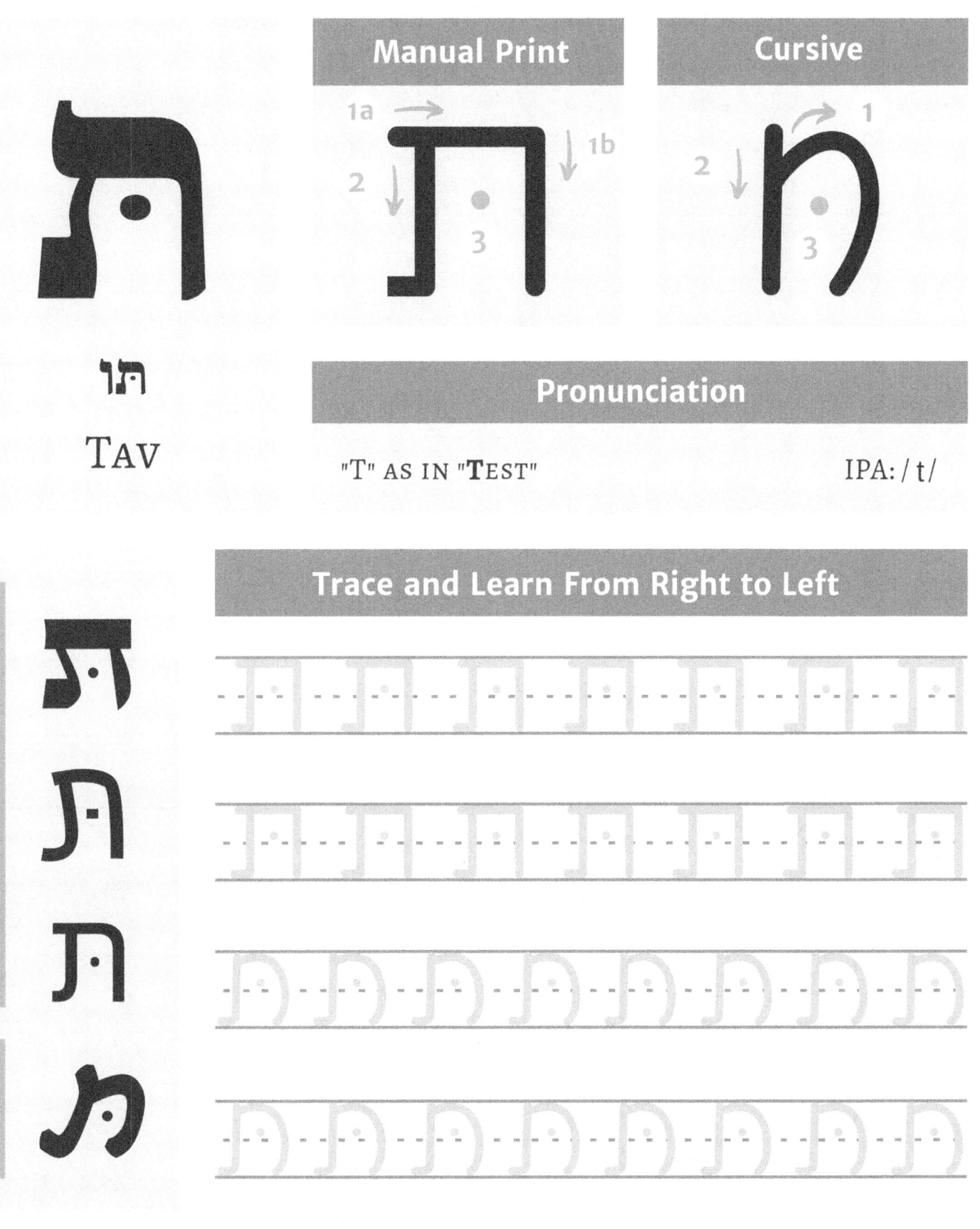

## Cursive

תו

TAV

## Pronunciation

"T" AS IN "TEST"

IPA: /t/

## Trace and Learn From Right to Left

## Manual Print

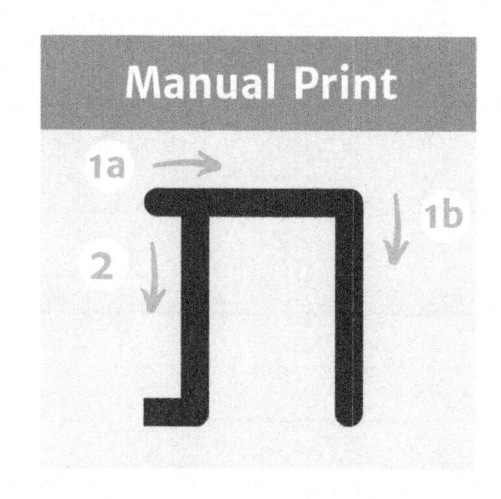

## Cursive

תו

TAV

## Pronunciation

"T" AS IN "TEST"

IPA: /t/

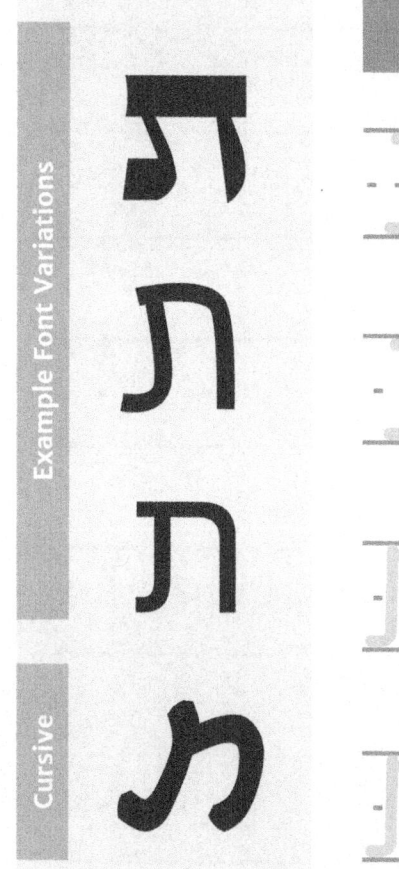

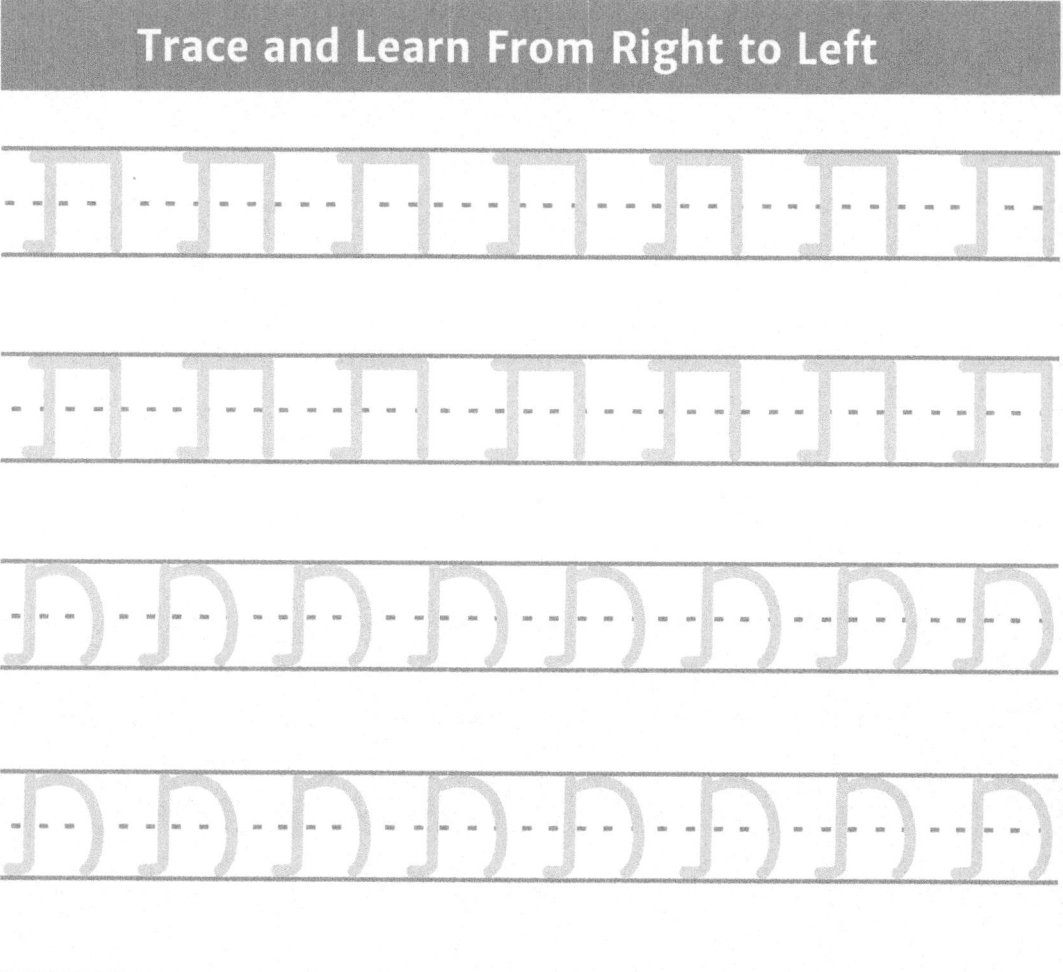

## Trace and Learn From Right to Left

**Example Font Variations**

**Cursive**

תתתתתתתתתתת

# Niqqud Diacritic Marks Reference Chart

Note: in this chart, א is used as the base consonant because it is silent. You can and should use other consonants in your handwriting practice.

| | | |
|---|---|---|
| **A/Ah (Long) or O/Oh (Short)** IPA: /ä/ or /ǫ/ | **A (Short)** IPA: /ä/ | **A (Very Short)** IPA: /ä/ |
| **E/Ei (Long)** IPA: /ẹ/ | **E (Short)** IPA: /ẹ/ | **E (Very Short)** IPA: /ẹ/ |
| **Ei/Ey (Long)** IPA: /j/ | **Ey (Long)** IPA: /j/ | |
| **I/Ee (Long)** IPA: /j/ | **I/Ee (Short)** IPA: /i/ | |
| **U/Oo (Long)** IPA: /u/ | **U/Oo (Short)** IPA: /u/ | |
| **O/Oh (Long)** IPA: /ǫ/ | **O/Oh (Very Short)** IPA: /ǫ/ | **O/Oh (Long)** IPA: /ǫ/ |
| **E (Vocal Short)** IPA: /ẹ/ or /∅/ | | |

In the following pages you'll find ample space to train your ability to handwrite these diacritic marks. Feel free to photocopy those pages as needed.

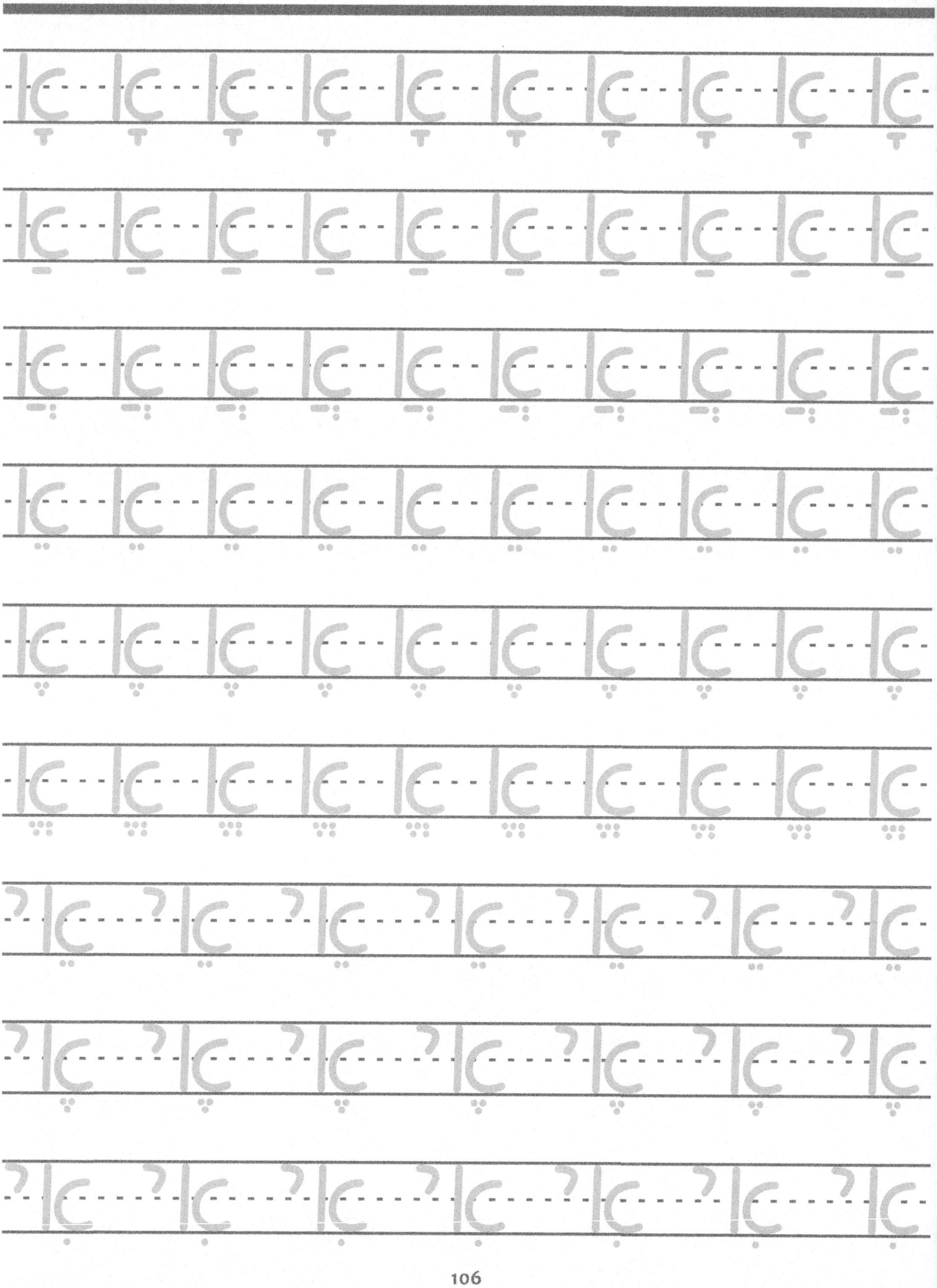

107

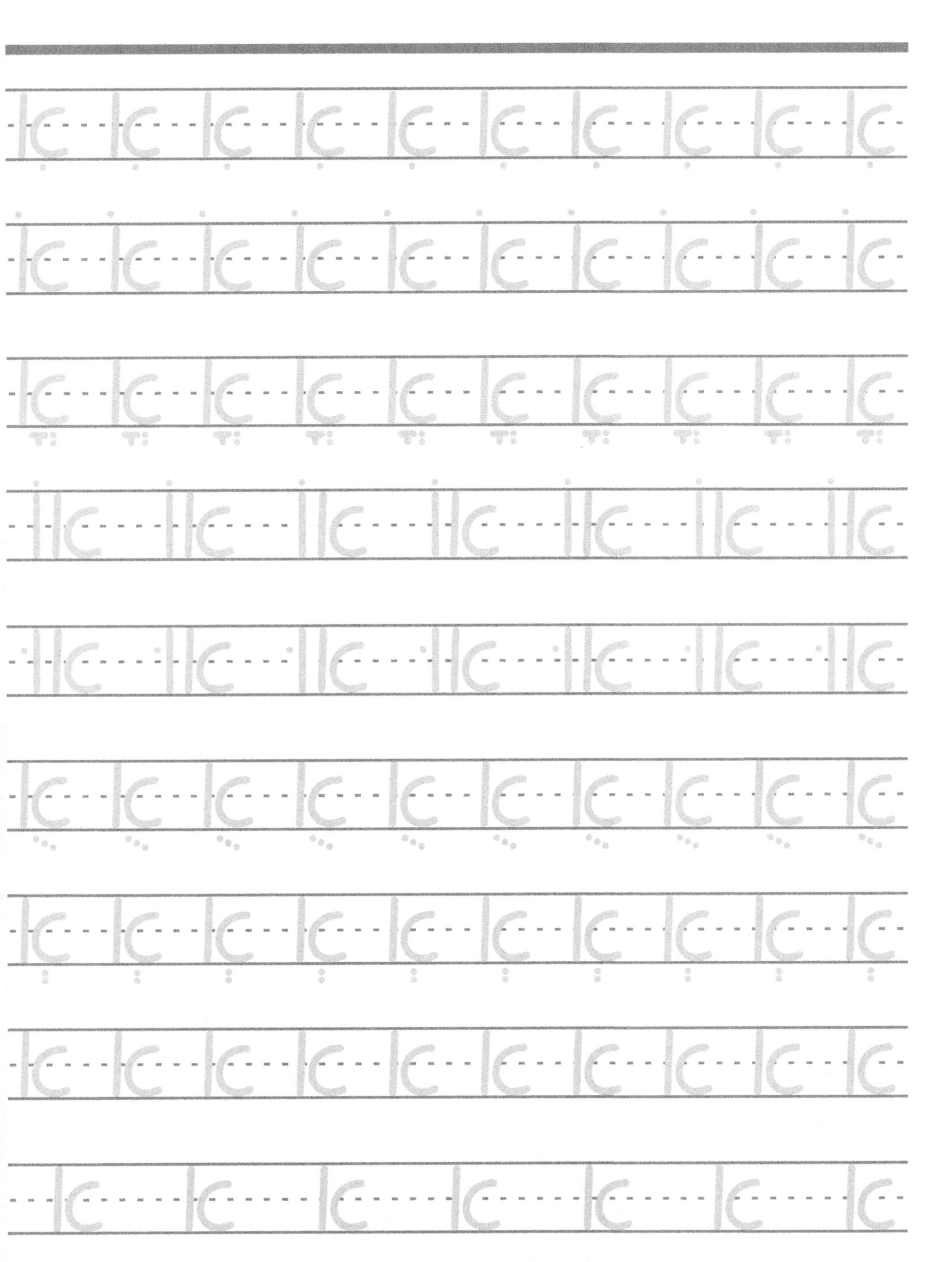

110

Made in the USA
Las Vegas, NV
21 June 2021